RICE & SPICE

RICE & SPICE

Rice Recipes from East to West

by Phyllis Jervey

Illustrations by M. Kuwata

Charles E. Tuttle Company

Rutland, Vermont
Tokyo, Japan

*Published by the Charles E. Tuttle Company
of Rutland, Vermont and Tokyo, Japan
with editorial offices at 15 Edogawa-cho,
Bunkyo-ku, Tokyo*

All rights reserved

*Library of Congress
Catalog Card No. 57-10198*

*First Printing, 1957
Third Printing, 1959*

*Printed in Japan
Toppan Printing Company*

For W. W. J.

whose ancestor planted
the first rice in America

CONTENTS

Preface	9
FROM THE EAST . . .	
India's Indispensable Rice	15
Ceylon's Celebrated Curry	22
Malay's Magic Touch	26
Javanese Rijsttafel	28
Philippine Perfection	34
Chinese Coolie Tiffin	38
Korean Specialty	44
Japan's Friendship Dish	46

... THROUGH THE UNITED STATES ...

Hawaiian Hospitality	55
California's Choicest	61
Texas Taste	77
Louisiana's Jambalaya	84
Kentucky's Burgoo	88
South Carolina's Gold	90
Washington Whirl	98
Minnesota Wild Rice	118

... TO THE WEST

Mexican Holiday	127
Canal Zone Casseroles	132
West-Indian Spanish Rice	138
Haitian Highlights	154
Jamaican Suckling Pig	161
Barbados Bounty	166
Trinidad's Melting Pot	172
Curaçao's Cuisine	181
Glossary of Spices	185
Index	195

PREFACE

Recently, at a women's luncheon, the subject turned to food, as it usually does. Someone flippantly mentioned "the dreary monotony of rice." To me this was a direct challenge.

With that succinct phrase in mind, I began the welcome task of proving that rice, if treated with respect and verve, can create remarkably exciting and unusual one-dish party and family meals. This book is the result, a sort of culinary cruise in which I have traced a voyage from East to West, from India, the first home of rice, through the United States, and finally on south of the border to the Caribbean.

What a tour of discovery this journey in search of rice and spice has become! The memories that I have so happily relived stem from our own gay tripping around the globe.

Though thanks are due to all the many helpful people I have met, I should especially like to thank the rice promotion associations for their ready cooperation in giving me information; the American Spice Trade Association for permission to use the Spice Glossary which appears at the end of this book; and the California Wine Institute.

From family and friends and from my own collection of recipes gathered at their sources, here is Rice & Spice for your pleasure.

First, a few basic directions for cooking rice:

It is not necessary to wash packaged rice. Modern rice is machine-milled and comes ready to be cooked. Cook rice in as little water as possible. It will retain more flavor and will have a better texture than if a large quantity of water is used. The method best known today is the "1-2-1" (1 cup rice, 2 cups water, 1 tsp. salt). For converted, minute, brown, or wild rice, follow directions on the packages.

When cooking rice for seafood dishes, substitute bottled clam juice with a touch of soy sauce and/or fresh lemon juice, for water; for Spanish or Mexican rice, use tomato or vegetable juice, or a blend of each; for chicken and seafood combinations, use half clam juice and half chicken broth; for meat dishes where rice is the basis, use canned consommé or bouillon. Plain salted water with a little butter added is of course an old reliable stand-by.

Rice can be flavored in other ways by adding to the boiling water garlic, onion, or celery salt (instead of regular salt) to taste, with 1 tsp. vegetable oil. One may also use paprika, curry powder, or turmeric (about ½ tsp.), depending on what flavor or color you seek. Chopped nuts give crunchiness to cooked rice, and a few raisins or currants with a sprinkling of ginger in the rice water make rice delicious with curried meats.

For further variation in exquisite flavoring, add 1 tbsp. fresh lemon or lime juice to 2 cups flaky, hot, cooked rice, with any combination of crushed sweet herbs to taste. This teams perfectly with broiled fish. Chopped green or ripe olives are a special addition to Spanish or plain rice and compliment a crisp pork roast. Rice prepared this way can be used as a stuffing. Grated lemon and orange rind combined with cooked wild or white rice goes with game or poultry of all kinds. Frozen cooked artichoke hearts, chopped and lightly sautéed in butter and sprinkled with paprika, add that gourmet fillip to wild or white rice. Stir the chopped artichoke hearts into hot, cooked rice. Top with several whole hearts and serve with creamy scrambled eggs for "bruncheon."

Boil rice gently at first, then reduce heat, and simmer. Rapid boiling may break the grains. Cover the pan tightly and do not peek during cooking. Depending on how dry or soft you prefer rice, cook from 14 to 20 minutes. Do not rinse after cooking.

In the recipes that follow I give various cooking methods used in other countries, but I find that packaged rice always insures smooth and separate grains. Rice is economical, as any leftover rice may be refrigerated and reheated by adding a little water and simmering over low heat.

Do you know that rice can be frozen? Properly cooked rice can be frozen and held as long as eight months. Any of the recipes in this book can be used with frozen rice as well as with freshly cooked rice. There is even a slight improvement in quality in the frozen rice. Thaw only as much as is needed at a time. Never refreeze thawed rice.

In the countries we will visit on our travels, we will find that rice is used in many ways—and even the water in which it is cooked is not wasted. The East Indians make a hot-weather beverage from plain, unsalted rice water (drained off after cooking rice), cooled and flavored with sugar, lemon, and orange juice. A shake of powdered ginger sparks it up.

FROM THE EAST...

INDIA'S INDISPENSABLE RICE

■ ■ ■ It is in India that we will start our journey searching for rice recipes, since, according to authorities, it was there in about 3600 B.C. that rice was first cultivated. The ancestor of the rice we enjoy today was a wild cereal-grass found in India in prehistoric times. It was the Greeks, during the expeditions of Alexander the Great, who first brought rice to Europe. In India it is used as part of religious rites.

India's rice is indispensable since more than half the world now depends on rice for nourishment. People of the East Indies are past masters, not only in the culture of their many species of rice, but especially in the subtle addition of spices to their inimitable rice cuisine.

East Indian gastronomy has traveled gracefully as far as the West Indies, where we will discover still more versions of Rice & Spice.

CHICKEN CURRY and RICE, CALCUTTA

1 chicken, 5 lbs.
Fresh ginger root
1 clove garlic
3 tbsps. curry powder
Shortening
3/4 cup flour
1 onion, sliced
White rice mounds, East Indian style
Sambals or side dishes

Serves 6. Disjoint chicken; fry delicately in hot shortening with onion and minced garlic in heavy skillet. Place in stewing kettle, cover with salted water, bring to a boil, then simmer until chicken is tender. Remove meat from bones. Keep warm. Mix curry powder and grated fresh ginger (or powdered ginger) with a little broth, add to chicken. Reduce this broth to 4 cups, blend flour (previously browned) with this, stir and cook until smooth. Pour over chicken and serve on a hot platter. Surround by steaming white rice, East Indian style, and pass *sambals* (side dishes) to be sampled at your guests' discretion.

White Rice, East Indian Style

2 cups long-grain rice
2 tsps. salt
2 tbsps. butter
5 cups water
1 tsp. lemon juice or mild white vinegar

Serves 6. Wash rice until starch is removed. Have boiling water ready in deep saucepan. Add salt, lemon juice, and butter. Drop rice in slowly, bring to a boil, cover, then simmer over low heat until rice is tender but not broken. Steam in colander over hot water. Cover rice with a clean cloth. The quality of native rice varies, which makes a difference in the amount of water to use. This is why I prefer to use packaged rice.

Sambals or Side Dishes

According to the number of condiments served with it, Curry and Rice is called "Eight-boy Curry," "Nine-boy Curry," or whatever number of side dishes you provide. Traditionally, in India each condiment was served by a different turbaned houseboy dressed in a white, starched, high-collared tunic. Generally, today, side dishes are passed on a revolving "Lazy Susan" tray. The steaming rice comes first, next the curry, then the sambals. I serve seven of these plus chutney, so mine is an "Eight-boy Curry" (minus the boys!).

Choose from the following: (1) Fresh, grated coconut (or thawed frozen, or canned dehydrated coconut can also be used). (2) Sliced, sautéed onion rings, browned and dried in hot oven (the frozen or canned style are easiest to use). (3) Chopped green and sweet red peppers (or cut-up canned pimientos) in a ring, the red in the center, surrounded by the green. (4) Small pieces of crisply fried, drained bacon. (5) Sieved, hard-cooked eggs, the whites around the edge of the dish and the yellow in the center. (6) Chopped peanuts. (7) Bombay dux (a species of East Indian dried fish, but any salty, dried fish such as kippered herring may be used). (8) Bananas, sautéed in butter to a golden brown, sprinkled with sugar, fresh lime juice, and grated nutmeg. (9) Chilled cucumbers with rinds left on, cut crosswise in thin slices and marinated in French dressing. (10) Freshly grated lemon and orange peel. (11) Chopped fresh parsley and chives. (12) Chopped, peeled, firm green and red tomatoes. (13) Seedless raisins or currants, soaked and drained. (14) Grapefruit segments soaked in sherry. (15) Slivered almonds, toasted. (16) The chutney may be homemade, or Major Grey's is always reliable.

Poppadum may be bought imported from India. These are fragile, rice-flour wafers used as bread. Any of the famous East Indian teas may be served at tiffin (lunch). A fruit sherbet cools the palate, which the rice foundation has already assisted nobly in doing.

LORD NAPIER'S CHUTNEY

9 small chili peppers
1/2 lb. raisins
4 cloves garlic
1 cup green or preserved ginger, sliced
1/2 lb. currants
1 lb. blanched almonds, chopped
2 qts. vinegar
1 tbsp. salt
1 tsp. red pepper
8 lbs. sugar
1/2 tsp. ground ginger
10 lbs. mangoes (after peeling)

Makes about 10 pints. Grind the chili peppers together with the almonds, raisins, currants, garlic, and ginger. Bring the vinegar and sugar to a gentle boil; continue boiling 15 minutes with the salt, red pepper, and ground ginger. Add sliced, peeled mangoes, cooking until fruit is tender, and watching for scorching. Seal in sterilized jars.

This recipe came to British friends of mine through Lord Napier when he was viceroy of India. It is very special and authentic.

2 lbs. mutton or veal
Salt to taste
1 cup sliced onions
1 clove garlic, minced
6 tsps. curry powder
1 cup grated coconut
1/2 cup pounded almonds
1 tsp. saffron or turmeric
Butter
1 tsp. ground ginger
2 tbsps. brown sugar
1 tsp. dried mint
1/2 tsp. ground cloves
1/2 cup cream or evaporated milk
Juice of two fresh limes
Hot white rice

BENGAL CURRY of MUTTON or VEAL

Serves 6. This is a famous old recipe given me by British friends. Mix the powdered ginger with the brown sugar. Whenever possible, use pounded fresh ginger. Add ½ stick of melted butter mixed with the mint. In India, "ghee," a rendered butter, is used. Season to taste with salt. Rub this mixture into the mutton (lamb) or veal. Be sure the piece is fat-free and top-grade. Cut the meat into thin slices and let stand 30 minutes. Meanwhile, sauté the onion lightly in hot butter but do not scorch. Put the seasoned meat into an earthenware saucepan, add garlic and curry powder according to preference—some like it hot, some do not. Cook meat in additional butter until nicely browned and cooked through, but still juicy. Add onions, grated coconut, cream or evaporated milk, almond paste, saffron or **turmeric**, lime juice, and salt. Cover closely and cook slowly 20 minutes. Add consommé if necessary. Serve in a beautiful rice ring with condiments of your choice.

EAST INDIAN CURRIED SHRIMP

2 lbs. fresh shrimp
1 piece green ginger, crushed
2 tbsps. lemon juice
1 stick butter (1/2 cup)
3 cups strained shrimp liquor
Salt, pepper, paprika
2 onions, sliced
1 clove garlic, minced
1 cup canned apple-sauce
2 cooked carrots and celery stalks, each puréed
2 tbsps. cornstarch
3 tbsps. curry powder
Ring of hot white rice
Condiments

Serves 6–8. This is my own adaptation of the Indian version. Steam unpeeled, fresh or frozen jumbo shrimp or prawn in colander over boiling water. Ten minutes should suffice, as the shrimp must still be firm. Save liquid. Cool shrimp, peel, and return shells to liquid, adding salt, garlic, and pickling spices. Simmer until a good broth is made, adding more water and a little Tabasco sauce to make the required 4 cups of liquid. De-vein shrimp, leaving whole. Make curry sauce by sautéeing onions and garlic very lightly. Add ginger, the canned applesauce, and vegetable purée. Stir in the combined curry powder and cornstarch with a little liquid. Gradually pour in the warm, strained shrimp liquor until a smooth sauce is formed. It should not be very thick, as curry has a tendency to thicken, especially if kept overnight in a refrigerator. This is one of the advantages of a curry: it improves its flavor to "stand." Making it in advance means that most of the work will have been done ahead of your party. The only last minute preparations will be reheating the curried dish over hot water and steaming the all-important rice. The condiments should also be arranged ahead of time, with the exception of the fried foods and eggs. To serve the curried shrimp, add them to the sauce 15 minutes before using, season, add fresh lemon juice if desired. Serve hot in center of rice ring.

Rice Ring

2 cups long-grain rice
2 tsps. salt
2 tsps. fresh lemon juice or white vinegar
4½ cups boiling water
2 tbsps. butter
Chopped parsley
White pepper

Serves 6–8. Cook rice as previously described (directions are on package of converted rice, which I prefer because of its retention of valuable vitamins and minerals). Add the pepper and parsley and pack into a well-buttered ring mold. Place it over hot water, covering with wax paper or foil. When ready to serve, unmold on warm chop-plate. Fill center with the curried shrimp. Sometimes, in getting the rice out, it helps to loosen the edges of the ring with a wet spatula.

CEYLON'S CELEBRATED CURRY

■ ■ ■ While in Colombo we were entertained by a wealthy Ceylonese tea planter at tiffin. He explained the secrets of true curry-making as he escorted us about his plantation: ingredients must be absolutely *fresh*. To prove his point, he told us that everything which we were about to taste was grown in his extensive tropical gardens, with the exception of the shrimp, which came straight from the sea, as Ceylon is an island independent of India. The curry powder is pounded daily from various fresh spices. Local curries are cooked in native *chatties* (cook pots) in a cookhouse usually separated from the main domicile.

Never had we tasted such curry! There was a white curry and a yellow curry, the latter being the stronger. "If your guests do not appreciate a sharp curry," our host told us, "you had better give them a bland or white curry. This is why we serve both." Curry, while usually hot to the palate, is cooling to the system. Refreshing Ceylon tea has a tongue-soothing effect.

CEYLONESE CURRY

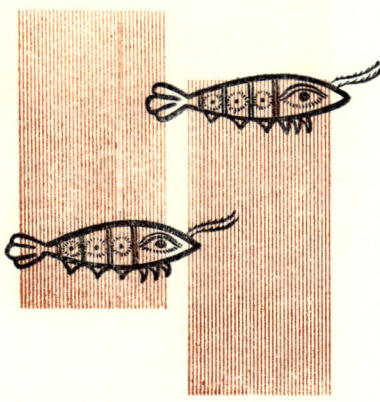

2 lbs. fresh shrimp
Crushed Canton ginger
White cornmeal
1 cup coconut milk
1 cucumber, peeled, seeded, and chopped finely
4 cups cooked, white rice
3 onions, sliced
2 cloves garlic, minced
Mixed fresh spices or 3 tbsps. best curry powder
Tamarind or fresh lime juice
Minced fresh mint added to butter

Serves 8. The shrimp were steamed for 10 minutes, drained, peeled, and de-veined. The shrimp liquor was seasoned and cooked with the shells, onions, garlic, salt, and peppercorns. When spicy, it was strained and a smooth sauce made with ½ cup cornmeal and the curry powder. Often a large, peeled, boiled white potato is mashed and used for thickening curries.

The ginger, salt, cucumber, and lime juice were added, followed by the whole shrimp. Coconut milk was added last and just heated through, but not boiled, to prevent curdling.

The curried shrimp were served on hot, cooked rice seasoned with ghee (rendered butter) flavored with mint. Eggplant slices delicately browned in oil with seasonings were also included.

FISH and RICE KEDGEREE

2 cups fish
1 bayleaf
Peppercorns
Salt
Lime juice
2 cups cooked rice
3 onions, sliced
1 clove garlic, minced
Red pepper, cayenne
Saffron or turmeric
Additional chopped onions, fried
Pimiento
Hard-boiled eggs, optional
Lentils, optional

Serves 6. Place raw, firm, white fish in enough water to cover. Add salt, peppercorns, bayleaf, 1 sliced onion, and lime juice. Simmer until just tender. Drain, cool, and remove bayleaf and peppercorns. Flake the fish, but not finely. Brown 2 remaining onions and garlic in butter with red pepper, and a little turmeric or saffron, and when onions are soft, add the rice, the fish, salt and pepper to taste, and a slight pinch of cayenne. Sauté until everything is lightly browned, but do not mash. Pass small bowls of fried, chopped onions, chopped crystallized ginger, and pimiento. Sliced hard-boiled eggs may be added at the last moment of cooking. Cooked dried lentils are also often included. A filling dish for "bruncheon."

This was once the English favorite when Ceylon was a British crown colony. Ceylon is an independent republic today. The natives call their version of lentils and rice *kitcheri*.

MALAY'S MAGIC TOUCH

■ ■ ■ "Without rice, nothing will succeed," says an old Malayan proverb. Their magic touch surely succeeds!

Only a curry connoisseur can detect the variations in different spices used in the famous curries of "monsoon" countries. A long-time British resident of what is now the Federation of Malaya gave me his favorite curry recipe. We found for ourselves that the Malayan curries are more delicately spiced than others. The white, flaky rice we are accustomed to is given a yellow glow with the addition of turmeric. Ginger is lovingly used, as is the sweet red pepper. Color and taste blend to create a magic cuisine, as much a part of Malayan life as are their beautiful orchids growing everywhere.

MALAY CHICKEN CURRY with RICE

4 lb. chicken, cut up
1/4 cup curry powder
1/2 tsp. powdered ginger
1 tbsp. flour
1 cup chicken broth
1 cup sliced mushrooms
Salt, pepper
1/2 cup diced celery
1/2 cup diced onions
Oil
Golden rice

Serves 4–6. Sauté onion, garlic, and celery in oil until tender. In separate skillet, brown the cut-up chicken in more oil, add sautéed vegetables, and cook slowly for about 1 hour, or until tender. Place broth in saucepan with mushrooms, curry powder, ginger, and flour. Heat gently. Add this mixture to chicken. When ready to serve, sprinkle soaked currants and grated coconut over top for a true Malayan touch. If possible, serve mangosteens as the dessert. Experts say that this is the queen of all fruits and compare its taste to strawberries and peaches and cream mysteriously compounded. Serve Malay chicken with golden rice, passed separately.

Golden Rice

Serves 4–5. To 3 cups steamed white rice, add 1 tsp. powdered turmeric, diluted with a little chicken broth; add 2 tbsps. melted butter; stir rice until lightly browned in a heavy skillet. Taste for seasoning. Minced chives, parsley, or shredded onion tops may be added. Pine nuts, chopped cashews or pistachios, or slivered, blanched almonds give a fine flavor to golden rice. Pineapple bits sautéed in butter also gives that extra something to the rice.

JAVANESE RIJSTTAFEL

■■■Few writers about Java have failed to make some reference to the famous Rijsttafel. The origin of this national gastronomical ritual goes back to the early days of the Dutch colonization of the Netherlands East Indies, over three hundred years ago. In those days, the pioneers had to live on the resources of the country, and with the Hollander's great liking and capacity for good food, they made the most of the material available. Rijsttafel was the astounding result.

At the Hotel des Indes in Batavia, we were served the Javanese Rice Table. Headed by the Number One Boy carrying a large chop-plate of fluffy rice piled high, some twenty or more native boys in sarongs and head kerchiefs followed in Indian file. Each balanced a filled dish in either hand. Using the essential rice as the base, something from all or any of the dishes was taken by the guests. These were placed around the rice in individual little mounds. The manager of the hotel gave me the following descriptions of some of the dishes on the menu.

RIJSTTAFEL

Sajoer Curry
Sambal Goreng Oedang
Rempejeh
Minced Shrimp Balls
Minced Indian-corn Balls

Sajoer Curry

1 chicken
Milk of one coconut
1 tamarind
4 chopped lichee nuts
1/4—1/2 tsp. saffron or turmeric
2 thin slices ginger or 1/2 tsp. powdered ginger
2 cloves garlic, minced
2 tsps. finely sliced chilies
1 tsp. coriander seeds
1/4 tbsp. Kümmel liqueur
Cabbage, shredded
Stringbeans, frenched
Eggplant, cut up
Green pepper, chopped

Serves 6–10, depending on appetites. Fry the spices in a little oil. Slice the chicken and brown with the spices. Add the Kümmel, a little water, and the vegetables. Steam together until done, then add 1 cup coconut milk. To obtain this milk, frozen, shredded coconut (available in the U.S.) can be used. Soak it in evaporated milk, then squeeze it through several layers of cheesecloth. The resulting liquid is a good substitute for the real thing. Although no curry powder is listed here, the same spices are found in regular curry powder, and the effect is similar to that of commercial curry powder, but somewhat stronger.

Sambal Goreng Oedang

2 cups shrimp, cut up	1 tsp. lemon-grass stem
1 tsp. minced garlic	(or grated lemon
4 tbsps. shallots or	peel)
green onions	Coconut milk
1 piece green ginger, chopped	1/2 tsp. red pepper
	Salt

Serves 6–10, depending on appetites. This is a highly seasoned side dish of shrimp. Pound together in a mortar the onions or shallots, garlic, ginger, lemon-grass stems or peel. Fry in butter or oil. Add the shrimp cut in small pieces, a little coconut milk, the red pepper, and salt to taste.

Rempejeh or Fried Peanuts

1 cup peanuts	Water
1 tsp. coriander seeds	Salt, pepper
1 clove garlic	1/2 cup spinach, chopped
Flour	
Egg	

Serves 6–10, depending on appetites. Grind peanuts through the medium blade of a food grinder. Make a batter of the water, egg, flour, spinach, salt, and pepper. Pound the coriander and garlic together in a mortar until fine. Add these with the peanuts to the batter. Make small cakes and fry.

Minced Shrimp Balls

2 cups cooked shrimp	Java pepper, salt, nutmeg
2 eggs, beaten	
1 clove garlic, minced	Parsley, minced
1/2 loaf bread	

Serves 6–10, depending on appetites. Mince the shrimp. Soak the bread in water, squeeze it dry, and break into fine particles. Mix shrimp, bread, the egg, and the rest of the ingredients. Make into little balls, fry in oil, and drain. They make fine cocktail fare.

Minced Indian-corn Balls

Young Indian corn
Spinach, chopped finely
1 egg, beaten
Java pepper, salt

Serves 6–10, depending on appetites. Grate the corn, and mix with spinach. Add the egg, salt, and pepper. Make small cakes and bake on a griddle.

Gin slings or Kuyper schnapps preceded this gargantuan banquet. Amstel beer helped extinguish the inner conflagration caused by the curry. Some simpler Javanese recipes follow in case you are not so ambitious as to try Rijsttafel.

JACHTSCHOTEL or CURRIED MEAT with RICE

Cook cut-up meat with chopped onions, soy sauce, butter, coconut milk, and curry powder to taste. When this comes to a boil, add some cornstarch mixed with a little milk, to make a thick sauce. Sprinkle with parsley. In a baking dish, first put a layer of curried meat, then a layer of cooked rice. Top with bread crumbs and dots of butter. The proportions will depend on the amount you need. This makes a delicious buffet supper dish with chutney.

AJAM BESENG or CHICKEN CURRY with RICE

1 chicken
2 onions
1 celery stalk
1 tbsp. curry powder
Salt, pepper, paprika
1 can bouillon
1 cup coconut milk
2 leeks
3 tiny chilies
Dry white rice

Serves 6. Steam chicken until half done. Put in oven, add salt and butter, and bake until cooked through and nicely browned. Make a sauce by first frying the diced onions, leeks, and celery, mixing in the mashed chilies and curry powder; then gradually add the bouillon and coconut milk. Cut chicken into medium pieces. Cover with the heated sauce. Serve on mounds of steaming white rice.

SATÉ with RICE or SKEWERED MEAT with RICE

1/2 lb. beef
1/2 lb. pork
1/2 lb. lamb

4 tbsps. soy sauce
Minced red chilies
Green pepper
3 tsps. hot water
1 tsp. vinegar
Grated onion
Oil
A little sugar
Hot rice

Serves 6. Cube the meat, then put six squares of each meat alternately on wooden skewers or sharpened bamboo sticks. Combine the other ingredients to make a sauce. Grill meat over charcoal until brown. Serve meat and sauce with bowls of steaming rice.

NASI GORING or FRIED RICE

2 cups cooked rice
1 cup shrimp, minced
2 onions, chopped
1 cup grated coconut
1 cup ground peanuts
Butter
Cubes of fried pork
1/2 lb. cubed, cooked ham
2 eggs
Salt, paprika
Tabasco sauce
Chopped parsley

Serves 4. Fry rice with butter, turning often until golden. Sprinkle paprika, a little Tabasco, and salt over all. Taste to see if sufficiently piquant. Fold in the cooked, minced shrimp, fried onion, pork, and ham. Leave in covered pan to keep warm. Brown coconut separately. Fry toasted peanuts, and place the coconut and peanuts each in side dishes. Beat eggs with 1 tsp. water and make into thin omelet. Fry until well done, and cut it into thin strips. Decorate the rice with them. After serving the fried rice, pass condiments. With cold beer or chilled wine and fresh pineapple, this is a delightful meal-in-itself.

PHILIPPINE PERFECTION

■ ■ ■ My most delightful memory of Manila is dining in the quadrangle of the old fort, the Bastille of Manila in the Spanish days. Our Army friends had dinner served on the ramparts. The Pasig River lapped at the foot of the high wall where rows of small fishing boats were moored. Masses of water hyacinths floated down from the jungle, and natives sang Tagalog songs to the accompaniment of soft guitars under a full tropical moon.

The following two recipes were given to me by U.S. Army Sergeant Leroy Black, one-time steward to General Pershing. They illustrate perfectly the Philippine love for and dependence on rice as a staple food. The rice is usually served with a sauce, not eaten plain as in Japan.

3 lbs. pork
2 cloves garlic
Juice of 1 lemon
10 whole cloves
1/2 tsp. nutmeg
1/2 tsp. ginger
1 small stick cinnamon
3 tbsps. vinegar
3 tbsps. olive oil
2 tbsps. paprika
Salt and pepper to taste
1/2 tsp. Accent
1 tbsp. peppercorns
Ring of white, flaky rice

PORK ADOBO

Serves 6. Cut meat in small pieces. Brown in oil; stir in minced, peeled garlic, the seasonings, and enough hot water to cover. Put in the lemon juice and grated rind, add vinegar, cover, and simmer 45 minutes. Stir often. Add more liquid if necessary. When pork is cooked through and tender, strain the sauce and reheat. It should cook down into a gravy-like consistency. Serve meat and some of the sauce in center of round platter. Surround with a ring of steamed rice. Pass extra sauce. This is a national favorite.

Rice Border or Ring

2 cups converted rice
4½ cups boiling water
2 tsps. salt
1/4 tsp. white pepper
2 tbsps. minced parsley
2 tbsps. butter

Serves 6. Start rice in boiling water, reduce flame, cover, simmer with 1 tsp. salt until water is absorbed. Add remaining salt, pepper, butter, and parsley, stirring with fork to blend. Turn into a well-buttered ring mold (1½ quart size) and pack rice so that it is firm. Place ring mold in pan of hot water. Heat over low flame 10 minutes. Unmold on platter.

PHILIPPINE PERFECTION

ROYAL CASSEROLE

4 tbsps. grated coconut
4 tbsps. chopped onion
1 clove garlic, minced
1 cup diced, boiled ham
1 cup tomato purée
8 breasts of chicken
1½ cups canned corn
1/2 cup sherry wine
1 green pepper, chopped
4 tbsps. hot olive oil
1 tsp. each salt and paprika
Border of white rice

Serves 8. Place the finely grated coconut (it comes frozen) and the whole corn niblets in a glass bowl, cover with the sherry, let soak. Sauté the onion, green pepper, garlic, and ham in the hot olive oil. Add the tomato purée, salt, and paprika. Next add the coconut, corn, and sherry. Heat through and when it begins to thicken, pour over 8 chicken breasts in baking dish. Cover and bake 1 hour at 325°. Serve on a heated round platter with a border of white, cooked rice, shaped into a ring with the back of a large spoon. Decorate with chopped parsley and pimiento. A tossed green salad; crisp, hard rolls; and, perhaps, iced champagne turn this casserole into a truly royal one.

■

Here is a **menu** typical of Philippine cuisine:

Persimmon and Avocado Cocktail
Chicken and Rice, Valenciana
Dry White Wine or Sherry
Palmito Salad with Tart Dressing
Fresh Coconut Ice Cream
Black Coffee   Liqueurs

CHICKEN and RICE, VALENCIANA

1 large hen
1/2 lb. ham, cut up
1 green pepper, chopped
Salt, paprika
2 cups tomato sauce
Water or chicken broth
1 tsp. powdered saffron
1 onion, chopped
1 clove garlic, minced
1 lb. ground pork
6 red Spanish sausages, sliced
2 cups raw rice
1 cup cooked crab meat or lobster
18 cooked prawn or large shrimp, peeled

Serves 8. Cut the chicken into serving pieces. Brown them in a large iron kettle or Dutch oven, in vegetable or olive oil. Add the onion, garlic, green pepper, tomato sauce, and enough hot water or chicken broth to cover. When the chicken is partly done, add the ground pork, sausage, and ham. Simmer until pork is no longer pink; then measure liquid, adding more broth (canned if desired), if necessary, to make 4 cups. Slowly add the rice, mix the saffron with a little of the hot broth, and stir into the rice and other ingredients. Cover tightly. Reduce flame and cook until rice is tender. Add the shrimp, crab, or lobster meat. Heat through and serve in a warm earthenware casserole with a cover. Have plenty of crusty French bread and chilled white wine for a satisfying one-dish meal.

Palmito is the heart of palm. It comes canned and is imported in the U.S.A. The dressing is made tart with chopped dill pickle and vinegar.

COOLIE TIFFIN

■ ■ ■ Rice has always played a leading role in China, where it is a staple food. A ceremony symbolic of its importance is said to have been established by a Chinese emperor in 2800 B.C., in which the emperor sowed the rice himself, while the seeds of four other kinds of grain were sown by princes of the realm. Rice has proverbially struck an important note in the civil, social, and religious ceremonies and observances of Oriental peoples. It was, and still is, the medium of exchange in many parts of the Orient. Debts, taxes, feudal obligations, and even wages have been paid in rice. The history of rice goes back into antiquity. The almost world-wide custom of throwing rice at newly married couples is known to be the survival of ancient religious practices of the Chinese and Hindus. In the Orient, rice is the symbol of fertility and throwing it at a newly wedded pair symbolizes the wish that they may be blessed with children. As the Oriental fairy tale relates: "Let your rice bowl be ever overflowing...."

■

CHINESE ALMOND CHICKEN with RICE

1/2 cup blanched almonds
1 tsp. salt
1 clove garlic, mashed
2 tbsps. each, liquid from bamboo and chestnut cans
3 tbsps. salad oil
1/2 cup water chestnuts, sliced
2 cups diced, cooked chicken
1 cup cubed bamboo shoots
1/2 cup sliced mushrooms, any kind

1 cup celery, thinly sliced
2 tsps. sugar
2 tsps. cornstarch
1/4 cup water
4 tbsps. soy sauce
1/2 cup green onions, sliced
3 cups hot, cooked white rice

Serves 6. Brown almonds in 1 tbsp. warm oil; do not burn. Drain and set aside. Place salt and garlic in a skillet with a tight-fitting lid. Mash peeled garlic into salt. Add 1 tbsp. oil, then the chicken. Brown lightly. Add another tbsp. oil, the bamboo shoots, and mushrooms. (If dried Chinese or Japanese mushrooms are used, soak first for several hours, draining and rinsing them.) Brown again lightly. Add liquid from bamboo shoots and water chestnuts. Cover skillet and cook over low heat for 5 minutes. Add water chestnuts, celery, and half the almonds. Heat through. Celery and chestnuts should stay crisp. Make a sauce by shaking in a jar with a lid the cornstarch, sugar, water, and soy sauce. Stir into the hot mixture. Cook until thickened and smooth. Serve over hot, cooked rice. Sprinkle rest of almonds and the green onions over top of each serving from separate little lacquer or porcelain bowls. Pass extra soy sauce.

This is a bountiful and exquisite repast, suitable for your most important party of the year.

■

CHINESE CHOPPED SHRIMP and VEGETABLES with RICE

1 lb. fresh shrimp
1 bunch celery
1/2 lb. pork
1/2 bunch green onions
Cornstarch
Watercress
1 head cauliflower, medium size
1 large can bamboo shoots
Soy sauce
Sugar, ginger
Olive oil
Dry, flaky rice

Serves 6. Boil the cauliflower in salted water until just tender and still firm. Drain. Cut into medium-sized pieces. Remove bamboo shoots from can, drain, and slice into pieces about 1 by 2 inches. Cut 1 bunch green (Pascal) celery into small, crosswise pieces. Clean the fresh shrimp and put to soak in soy sauce with a little sugar and some crushed green ginger (use powdered ginger if it is easier). Cut the pork into small pieces. Cut green onions into strips 1 inch long. Do not cook anything excepting cauliflower until almost ready to serve. Fry bamboo shoots and celery in a little olive oil (they may be done together), remove from fire. Fry pork until brown and cooked. Add the shrimps to cook through, but keep whole and firm. Season everything with the soy marinade, add a little water, and thicken with cornstarch (lightly). Add vegetables, heat well, and serve at once on heaped-up mounds of white, dry, flaky rice.

To prepare another version of Almond Chicken, the same ingredients as above are used with the exception of the shrimp and cauliflower. One cup mushrooms and ½ lb. blanched almonds are substituted. All vegetables and meat must be thinly sliced, or cut into small cubes with a very sharp knife. Nothing is *ever* put through the meat grinder in China. Cook the Almond Chicken as indicated in this shrimp recipe. Just before serving, add sliced, blanched almonds. Dry, flaky rice is a must.

Preserved kumquats, jasmine tea, and rice wafers complete a fine copy of a real Chinese dish. Chinese feasts have up to fifty courses and continue for hours. But one dish, such as either of the two just mentioned, will do an American family, or party, very satisfactorily. We call these our "Rice Dinners."

■

Fried Rice
Chicken with Vegetables
Vegetables with Ham

COOLIE TIFFIN

Fried Rice

Boil white rice until very dry, sauté it in peanut oil, add minced parsley and chives. Drain, serve hot. Amount to be used depends on number of people.

Chicken with Vegetables

Steam thawed frozen chicken until cooked through. Cool, then slice in strips with a very sharp knife. Brown lightly in oil with bamboo shoots; green celery, steamed first, then sliced across; chopped onion tops; soaked and drained Chinese mushrooms, sliced; blanched almonds (or walnuts); minced garlic. Cook everything until done but still very crisp. Amount to be used depends on number of people.

Vegetables with Ham

Sauté together in a little oil: frozen, frenched stringbeans, previously steamed until barely tender, and cut in halves; strips of well-done fried eggs; crumbled, crisply fried bacon; strips of boiled ham; minced garlic; and chopped green onions, including the tops. Cook until everything is heated through but not overdone. Amount to be used depends on number of people.

■

When our friends, General and Mrs. Willard G. Wyman, lunch alone, Chinese tea is the only accompaniment. Three dishes of Canton china filled with the above recipes, flanked by a bottle of soy sauce at either end, are placed on a bare table. When they have guests, their Chinese cook insists on adding chicken broth in which fresh eggs have been whisked and soy sauce added for seasoning. This first course is served in the same bowls to be used later for the main course of "Three Bowls." Grapefruit baskets, filled with assorted fruits soaked in sherry, are presented to each guest for dessert by the smiling chef.

The General has this same Coolie Tiffin every day that he is home, and never tires of it. Mrs. Wyman prefers a fruit salad as a variation. But we were in favor of the General's choice. Lucky any coolie ever to have such a feast! The Wymans were stationed in China for four years and certainly know their Chinese food. All of these Chinese rice dishes were given me by General and Mrs. Wyman for your delectation and mine.

KOREAN SPECIALTY

■ ■ ■ In the countryside in Korea, the fox is recognized as the God of Rice. It is he who is said to have carried the first rice seed on his tongue from Korea to Japan. These two countries have rice as a common denominator, and their native dishes are based on fish and rice. One of the everyday dishes upon which the country people of Korea subsist is "Pah Jook," their version of rice and beans, which we so often encounter on our travels from East to West.

Another very popular dish is made from *keem*, a local seaweed which is steamed and seasoned with soy sauce, with cooked rice folded in to form a substantial dish. Most Americans balk at seaweed, so I will omit details on this locally enjoyed item.

PAH JOOK or RICE and BEANS

1 cup kidney-type beans
1 cup rice
Salt to taste
Water to cover
1 onion
1 clove garlic
2 tbsps. peanut oil

Serves 6. The beans are soaked overnight and the next day they are simmered with onion, garlic, and salt in the same water until soft enough to mash through a colander. This purée is then fried in the peanut oil. The rice is washed and cooked in 2 cups boiling, salted water, then simmered with cover on for about 20 minutes, or until rice is tender and dry. The bean purée and the rice are mixed together with a little beef stock (or canned consommé). This is served hot with small dumplings made (in the U.S.) from packaged biscuit mix.

KOREAN CHICKEN

Chicken breasts
Soy sauce
White wine
Chopped green pepper
Mustard
Mashed ginger
Garlic
Cooked rice

A dish which we might like to serve is this Korean Chicken. Chicken breasts are marinated in soy sauce, white wine, chopped green pepper, mustard, mashed ginger, and garlic. They are broiled with oil, and served on the ever-present dry white rice with the heated marinade. Allow 1 whole breast or more per person.

KOREAN SPECIALTY

JAPAN'S FRIENDSHIP DISH

■ ■ ■ In Japan, as in all other Oriental countries, rice is the mainstay of the people's diet. One of my earliest recollections of rice is of my Japanese amah rolling cooked rice around a pickled plum or quince to form rice balls. These were special picnic fare with pots of steaming tea. The Japanese love these rice balls, kept moist with the "stuffing" of pickled fruit. Rice takes the place of bread or other starches in Japan and is to the Oriental what potatoes are to the European—the Staff of Life.

The Japanese wash their rice thoroughly and put it into a heavy pot, adding water to cover. As the rice varies, it is difficult to give the precise amount of water. Salt is not used, as soy sauce replaces it at the table. Contrary to

American custom, the rice is soaked for 2 hours, then brought to a fast boil; next the flame is turned low for 10 minutes. The fire is turned still lower for an additional 10 minutes. Then the heat is turned off entirely and the rice stands for 10 minutes more. It is closely covered throughout and never disturbed.

There are many ways of preparing the white rice so as to make very palatable one-dish meals. Red Rice is rice boiled with red beans, soy, and sesame seeds. Chestnut Rice is rice boiled with peeled chestnuts, soy, and their famous rice wine known as *saké*. In this country we substitute sherry or sauterne for saké. It is always served hot in small cups without handles.

I am giving only the better-known Japanese main rice dishes which our Service people have enjoyed while stationed in Japan. These recipes are simplified for American tastes. For authentic Japanese cookery in its entirety, you should have *Japanese Food and Cooking* by Stuart Griffin.

CHICKEN LEGS TERIYAKI on RICE

3/4 cup Kikkoman soy sauce
1/2 tsp. ginger
1 clove garlic, minced
Juice of 1 lemon
Grated lemon rind
Cooked white rice
12 chicken legs

Serves 4. Serve three small chicken legs apiece. I use frozen ones. Defrost and soak several hours in a sauce made of the first five ingredients. Bake in shallow pan in 325° oven, turning several times while cooking to brown evenly.

Baste with the sauce. Serve on a mound of hot white rice mixed with minced chives and parsley. The chicken legs are dressed in paper "papillotes," so that they may be picked up and eaten without benefit of knife or fork. Excellent for cocktail party fare.

TOKYO TEMPURA SHRIMP with RICE

12 fresh or frozen prawns, or jumbo shrimp
1/2 medium-sized eggplant (in strips)
Cauliflower buds
Large, fresh spinach leaves
Onion rings
Asparagus tips
Grated white radish
2 lobster tails, in chunks
Scallops or clams
Tempura batter
Tempura sauce
Cooked white rice
Lemon wedges
Ground ginger

Serves 4. Arrange the vegetables and cleaned, peeled shrimp and other seafood on large platter. Put electric skillet in center of table, fill with vegetable oil to 1½ inch in depth, and set temperature control at 400°. Or use an ordinary large skillet and cook on your stove, bringing the hot, drained food to the table as quickly as possible. Dip ingredients individually into the tempura batter, covering each completely. Fry quickly in the hot oil until lightly brown on each side. Cook everything about 3 minutes, except spinach, which needs only a moment. Drain on absorbent paper to remove excess oil. Dip piping hot, cooked pieces into tempura sauce. If clams are used, they should be chopped (use canned ones, drained and added to batter with a little chopped chives, ½ cup clams to 1½ cups batter). I use frozen breaded, fantail shrimp, ready to sauté quickly in hot oil until golden-hued for expeditious tempura, American style. Frozen, fried onion rings and frozen vegetables (all defrosted and patted dry) save time and work. Pass lemon wedges. The vegetables require batter, but the breaded shrimp or fried onions do not.

Tempura Batter

1 egg yolk
1/2 tsp salt
3/4 cup sifted flour
3/4 cup water or milk

Beat the yolk and water with fork or chopsticks in a bowl until mixed. Add flour and salt, stirring only until blended. Do not over-whip.

Tempura Sauce

1/4 cup Kikkoman soy sauce
1 tbsp. white wine
1/2 tsp. ground ginger
1/2 cup water
1 tsp. sugar
Grated white radish
Green onions, sliced thinly

Grated *daikon* (long white radishes) or horseradish, together with some thinly sliced green onions, add flavor and color to the above sauce. Mix the soy sauce, wine, water, sugar, and vinegar. Sprinkle radish and/or onions into mixture, each to his own taste, after the sauce has been warmed and poured into individual dipping bowls. We have some Satsuma ones acquired in Japan. Always serve tempura with side-bowls of hot, cooked rice. Chopsticks are gay but usually difficult for Occidentals to use. We find ourselves using our fingers most of the time, so finger bowls and many paper napkins are necessary. The rice may be eaten with porcelain spoons by the chopstick-shy. Kumquats, persimmons, quince, plums, cherries, tangerines, and pomegranates finish off this popular Japanese meal. Steaming fragrant tea is the accepted beverage along with saké. Heated, dry white wine or a dry white sherry will answer the purpose of saké in this country.

SUKIYAKI and RICE

1½ lbs. beef sirloin, sliced 1/8 inch thin
2 onions, sliced thin
1 bunch green onions
1 cup fresh or canned mushrooms, sliced
1 bunch watercress
1/2 to 1 cake of tofu (bean cake), cut into small blocks
4 green pepper slices, cut diagonally in 1/2 inch pieces
1 cup thinly sliced bamboo shoots
1 package frozen, frenched string-beans, cut across
1 cup shredded Oriental cabbage (long kind)
Sukiyaki sauce
Rice

Serves 4. The Japanese take such pride in presenting their foods with charming artistry. Arrange the sliced, fresh vegetables and meat ahead of time on an attractive platter and keep refrigerated. Place your hibachi, if you are fortunate enough to own one of these Japanese charcoal-burning braziers, in the middle of dining table. Usually, low tables on the order of coffee or cocktail tables are used. Guests then sit cross-legged on cushions on the floor around the table. Or use an electric skillet, or a rather heavy pan, large enough to hold everything, over a hot plate. The main idea is to cook while eating so that fresh, hot sukiyaki is always ready. Also if one prefers the meat rare, or the onions on the raw side, it can be prepared right at the table to individual order.

Melt some suet in pan and quickly cook vegetables, excepting watercress. Turn the vegetables. Add the meat and sauté with half of the sukiyaki sauce and a little water. Add cleaned watercress sprigs. No ingredient should cook long, as crispness is desired. This native stew is *always* combined with steaming, hot white rice, which is served in individual rice bowls. Each person helps himself from the main dish. The sukiyaki is served along with the rice. Add extra sukiyaki sauce for the necessary moisture. Chopsticks are used both for mixing while cooking and for eating. Chicken Sukiyaki is prepared in the same manner by adding boned, sliced chicken. Matsutake, the mountain mushrooms available in cans from Japan, may replace the other varieties.

This dish is usually served with a fresh raw egg, beaten with a fork or chopsticks, never an egg beater. The egg is placed in individual bowls and the hot sukiyaki is dipped into it before it is eaten. Use Accent instead of the Japanese Ajinomoto to emphasize flavor. Sukiyaki is called the "Friendship Dish" because of its great popularity with East and West alike.

Sukiyaki Sauce

- 1/2 cup Kikkoman soy sauce
- 2 tbsps. dry white wine or sherry, instead of saké
- 1/2 cup beef or chicken stock
- 4 tbsps. sugar

The amount of sugar may be slightly increased to taste. Mix the above together and let stand before using. This authentic soy sauce, known by the trade name of Kikkoman, is fabricated in Japan. It is scientifically prepared and aged 18 months before processing. It is a true soy sauce and adds the unique flavor so necessary to Japanese cookery. It is imported in the U.S.A. and I would not do without it, as it is a multi-purpose sauce. It may be bought in Oriental stores or ordered from the Kikkoman International in San Francisco.

...THROUGH THE UNITED STATES...

HAWAIIAN HOSPITALITY

■ ■ ■ From our friend Don Blanding's gay book of verse, *Vagabond House* (quoted by permission of Don Blanding and Dodd, Mead and Co., Publishers), comes the following apt description of a Hawaiian Curry.

> Lobster curry on mounds of rice...
> If you like curry it's mighty nice
> With grated coconut, feathered down,
> Little green onions frizzled brown,
> Nuts, and the yolks of hardboiled eggs,
> Mango chutney and garlic pegs,
> Anchovy paste and Bombay 'duck',
> Bits of bacon and Hindu truck,
> Minced green peppers and chowchow, too,
> And everything else that occurs to you!

As this lilting little poem indicates, imagine trying to eat a curried dish without rice as the supreme necessity—as the bland foil to absorb the spicy, tongue-sizzling sauce and condiments. Curries are especially suited for modern "do ahead" main-course luncheons, suppers, or buffets. With the addition of a sherbet, tea or other beverage, curry and rice are exotic meals-in-themselves.

CURRY in a COCONUT and RICE in a PINEAPPLE SHELL

Serves 4. With cleaver strike a large, fresh coconut (just turning yellow) a sharp blow, 1 inch from the top. The man of the house had best attend to this. Remove top, drain out coconut water, saving it for the sauce. Leave coconut jelly in the shell and fill it with curried seafood or meats of your choice. I suggest curried chicken with almonds and raisins; curried lobster, crab, or shrimp in combination or each alone; or any white, firm fish in good-sized pieces. Follow the recipe given for Honolulu Lobster Curry, adding the coconut water, with perhaps a little thickening. Return top to coconut and seal with a paste made from flour and water. Wrap each coconut completely in double tinfoil, put in pan filled half full with water. Bake in hot oven. After an hour, remove foil and serve curry from coconut shell right at the table. Pass the all-important rice in scooped-out fresh pineapple halves, foliage left on. With the pineapple flesh make an Island Fruit Compote by combining the cut-up pineapple, some papaya, mango, and bananas doused in sherry or brandy, and serve on fresh coconut ice cream. This menu is my own invention.

2 lbs. fresh shrimp
2 tbsps. curry powder
2 cups shrimp broth
Ginger, salt, paprika
Parsley
3 cups cooked rice
2 onions, sliced
1 clove garlic, minced
2 tbsps. butter, melted
Vegetable oil
Pimiento
Bacon

CURRIED CASSEROLE, WAIKIKI

Serves 6. Boil shrimp in seasoned water, remove them, peel, and throw shells back into same water. Make a highly seasoned broth as in East Indian Curried Shrimp. Sauté onion and garlic in oil, add curry powder and then broth gradually. Return shrimp to broth. Mix rice with melted butter. Line bottom of casserole with some of the dry, flaky white rice. Fill with shrimp and broth mixture, top with rest of rice. Sprinkle crumbled, sautéed bacon, chopped parsley, and canned pimiento over all. Heat thoroughly in moderate oven. Have condiments ready in small porcelain bowls, pass on round bamboo tray, with individual porcelain spoons. I used the rice-pattern bowls and spoons.

This was my solution for after-swim bruncheons at Waikiki, where we relaxed in an ocean-front cottage during part of our tour. This simplified service is a boon to any hostess, since curry and rice (that happily mated pair) remain faithful without dispute. The casserole may be cooked, cooled, and refrigerated the day before the party, reheated an hour before serving. Lump crab meat, lobster, or cooked, firm, fresh fish, such as salmon or tuna (or the canned variety may also do) is excellent fare. No bread is needed. Iced, minted tea was served, and juicy mangoes were eaten "out-of-hand," in our swim suits! Aloha!

'CURRY in a HURRY'

1 chicken, 4 lbs., cut up
1/2 tsp. powdered ginger
1/2 tsp. dried tarragon
1 cup sweet gherkins, sliced thinly
Salt, white pepper
Shortening
1 cup flour
1 clove garlic
2 tbsps. curry powder
Sherry or white wine
1 small can crushed pineapple
Chopped fresh mint
Border of white rice

Serves 6. This is a hurried but perfectly delicious inspiration of Hawaiian friends of ours. Unexpected guests were arriving for lunch (a military transport was in, friends were bringing friends!). So..."Shake chicken in brown paper bag containing flour, tarragon, salt, pepper, powdered ginger, and curry powder until each piece is well coated. Brown cut-up chicken with garlic quickly in hot shortening, using heavy iron skillet. Add gherkins and the crushed pineapple, including juice. Add canned chicken broth until it comes within one-fourth of the way to the top of skillet. Cover tightly, simmer one hour, turning chicken once or twice. Add sherry or white wine to taste. Serve very hot, on big chop-platter with a border of hot rice." For condiments use whatever you have on hand or, as Don Blanding says, "everything else that occurs to you!" If you should happen to have white seedless raisins, green seedless grapes, grated fresh coconut, fried bacon bits, sliced bananas soaked in fresh lime juice, guava jelly, and toasted nuts as our hostess had that memorable "Transport Day," by all means serve them with gusto as she did. How we looked forward to those happy interludes when we saw old friends and made new ones, as they passed through Honolulu during the three years we were stationed there.

HONOLULU LOBSTER CURRY

3 cups lobster meat
1 onion, chopped
1 clove garlic
2 cups coconut milk
Salt, white pepper
Cayenne
1 cup grated coconut
2 tbsps. curry powder
1 piece green ginger
1 tbsp. cornstarch
1/2 cup fried bacon bits
Lemon juice

Serves 6–8. Make a sauce from grated coconut heated in milk and allow to stand. Wring through double thickness of cheesecloth. Thicken with cornstarch and curry powder, mixed. Add sautéed onion and garlic. Strain through sieve, put into Pyrex casserole. Add precooked lobster chunks. Season, add piece of ginger, which must be removed before serving. Bake until heated through and sauce is right consistency. At serving time, sprinkle bacon bits over top.

Serve from casserole onto rice mounds, made by using a large coffee cup to mold the mounds. For condiments with a Hawaiian touch, serve: preserved pineapple slices; pieces of preserved ginger; chopped macadamia nuts; egg omelet, hard cooked; barley sprouts marinated in French dressing; anchovies; and mango chutney. Pass quartered fresh limes. A genuine Oriental curry is made without thickening. The

Hawaiian coconut is so meaty that the liquid becomes thick as cream after 2 hours of simmering. The nuts in the United States, however, are rarely so perfect, and the milk will not thicken without flour or cornstarch. To keep coconut milk from curdling, simmer gently; do not boil.

To "milk" dried coconuts, thrust an icepick into the "eyes," strain out milk. Crack open coconut; grate the coconut flesh, which in a dry coconut is hard. In Hawaii they have special graters for this purpose. Let coconut meat stand in its own milk with enough canned milk to make 2 cups milk to 1 cup grated coconut. Fresh cream may be used instead of the canned. Squeeze through two or more layers of cheesecloth.

There is an unsweetened commercial coconut cream on the market, much used in drinks. It is very good for curry sauces as well. This saves a lot of trouble. Of course most of us do not have coconut trees in our back or front yards, nor small native boys to climb them!

CALIFORNIA'S CHOICEST

■ ■ ■California always does everything in the most progressive way: the enormous and fertile rice fields in the Sacramento Valley are now planted by low-flying airplanes. Here too is one of the world's most modern rice mills.

California means Carmel to me. This town is on the history-steeped Monterey Peninsula and is now my parents' home. What pleasant family patio parties we have there—always Spanish dishes with rice and more rice! To counteract, we have a citrus salad, Carmel style, from the olive-hued lettuce with darkish red border, called "red lettuce" (properly named "Romano"), and tangerines, grapefruit, and avocado. Fish abound in Monterey Bay. It is a heavenly spot and the food is divine.

We often have Spanish suppers at haciendas of old Monterey families. One of the liveliest was given before the annual costume "Ball of the Eggshells" ("El Baile de los Cascarones"). Countless delicate eggshells are expertly filled with multicolored confetti and are the highlight of the *baile*. In colonial times, the don's custom was to crush these shells above his *favorita*'s mantilla-covered head. As the *cascarones* were delicately perfumed, the señoritas loved this romantic gesture. What a lovely memento to retain, this gay Monterey fiesta with so much life and color!

■

CRAB MEAT in RICE PATTIES

1 cup crab meat
Juice 1/2 lemon
1 can tomato soup
1 cup raw rice
Ripe olives
1/2 cup bread crumbs
1 onion, minced
1/2 cup milk
Salt, pepper
Mace, paprika
Pimiento

Serves 4. Add the bread crumbs to canned, fresh, or thawed frozen crab meat. Season with salt, pepper, paprika, ground mace, lemon juice, and minced onion. Turn condensed tomato soup into a saucepan, add milk and the seasoned crab meat. Heat slowly in double boiler. Cook rice in boiling, salted water at first; then simmer, covered, until tender; and drain. Shape rice into mounds on platter or individual plates, using back of large spoon. Make depression in center of each mound to form nests. Fill with crab meat mixture. Garnish with sliced, pitted, ripe olives, and pimiento.

CALIFORNIA POT ROAST of CHICKEN with BURGUNDY and RICE

4 tbsps. bacon drippings
1 hen, 4 or 5 lbs.
2 cups chicken broth
1/2 cup Burgundy wine
1 clove garlic, crushed
1½ cups raw white rice
2 tbsps. dry sherry
2 stalks celery, chopped
2 tbsps. parsley, chopped
6 carrots, sliced
1 (8 oz.) can tomato paste
1 onion, sliced
1 cup cooked frozen peas
Salt, pepper, paprika
Additional wine and broth

Serves 6. Heat bacon drippings in a Dutch oven or other heavy skillet, add cut-up chicken, and sauté until nicely browned on all sides. Add chicken broth, tomato paste, California Burgundy wine, onion, garlic, celery, parsley, and seasonings. Bring to a boil, then simmer until chicken is tender. Add more chicken broth and wine as it evaporates. There should be 3 cups liquid when you add the carrots and rice. Cover and cook until rice and carrots are tender. The liquid should be absorbed and the rice dry. Add sherry and peas. Heat carefully before serving.

Cooking time is shortened if chicken is cooked until almost tender in pressure cooker. Measure 3 cups broth and Burgundy, add seasonings, tomato paste, vegetables, and rice. Cook until rice and vegetables are tender and liquid is absorbed. Add sherry and peas.

Serve with hearts-of-artichoke salad on shredded lettuce. These tiny artichoke hearts come bottled in French dressing.

CHICKEN CURRY CALIFORNIA with RICE

1 stewing chicken (4 to 5 lbs.)
1 cup California sauterne wine
Several sprigs parsley
1 stalk celery
A few peppercorns
Salt to taste
6 tbsps. butter
2 tbsps. minced onion
2 tbsps. curry powder
1/2 cup flour
1½ cups milk
2 cups chicken broth
1/4 tsp. sugar
2 tbsps. California sherry
Hot rice ring

Serves 6. Place chicken in a large kettle. Add sauterne and enough boiling water so chicken is barely covered. Add parsley, celery, peppercorns, and salt. Bring to a boil, then cover and simmer gently for about 3 hours, or until chicken is tender. Let cool in broth, then remove meat from bones and cut in fairly good-sized pieces. Strain broth, skim off excess fat, add water, if necessary, to make required 2 cups. Prepare sauce as follows: melt butter, add onion, and sauté until limp and golden. Blend curry powder and flour; add milk and the 2 cups chicken broth; cook, stirring until mixture thickens and is smooth. Add sugar and salt. Add chicken to sauce and cook, covered, in a double boiler for about 30 minutes before serving. Just before bringing to table, add sherry. Pour into hot rice ring.

Condiments with a California touch are: (1) Bottled or canned tiny artichoke hearts, some pickled and some in French dressing. (2) Chopped ripe olives. (3) California sardines flavored with angostura bitters. (4) Tiny avocados minus seeds, a local variety, tender and sweet—peel just before serving, slice, and sprinkle with fresh lime or lemon juice, salt, and paprika. (5) Grapefruit, tangerine, and orange segments soaked in apricot brandy. (6) Raw zucchini unpeeled, sliced thinly, served crisp and "garlicked" (this means either sprinkled with garlic salt or powder, or dressed with olive oil in which several peeled, sliced garlic cloves have reposed. (7) Sultana raisins. (8) Seedless grapes. (9) Chopped fresh or dried figs or apricots, almonds, walnuts, and dates.

Needless to say a salad or dessert is totally out of place, but California sauterne is a delightful accompaniment. Always serve chilled, unless it is taking the place of the rice wine, saké; then it is served hot.

■

THE ADMIRAL'S PACIFIC PORK CHOPS with RICE

6 thick loin pork chops
6 thick slices onion
6 tbsps. raw rice
6 thick slices tomatoes
Sage, marjoram, salt, Java pepper
3 cups dry white wine

Serves 6. Brown chops in hot fat in skillet. Put them in shallow baking pan. On each chop, sprinkle powdered sage, marjoram, salt, and cracked Java pepper. Put a tablespoon of raw rice on each chop, cover each first with the onion slice, then with the sliced tomato. Pour the wine around the chops, cover pan, and bake in a moderate oven 350° for 2 hours. Serve with applesauce, hot date muffins, and chilled California sauterne. If an additional vegetable is desired, serve hot, cooked artichokes with Hollandaise sauce.

CRAB MEAT and RICE au GRATIN

2 cups raw white rice
4 tbsps. butter
4 tbsps. flour
1½ cups milk
1 (4 oz.) can mushrooms
1 cup grated Cheddar cheese
2 tbsps. pimiento
1/2 tsp. Worcestershire sauce
1/2 cup sherry
Salt, celery salt, pepper
2 cups crab meat

Serves 6. Cook rice until tender, according to directions on package. Melt butter; stir in flour; add milk and mushrooms, including liquid; cook and stir until mixture boils and thickens. Add half of the cheese, stir over low heat until melted. Remove from heat, add dry California sherry, minced pimiento, and seasonings. Combine cooked rice, crab meat, and sauce; mix lightly. Turn into greased casserole, sprinkle top with remaining cheese. Bake at 350° for 25 minutes until bubbly and delicately browned. This may be prepared the day before, kept refrigerated, and baked before serving. Serve with an avocado, grapefruit, and white seedless grape salad, sprinkled with pine nuts and French dressing on red lettuce.

RICE and RAISIN PUDDING for CHILDREN

1/2 cup cream or top milk
2 cups milk
1 tsp. vanilla
Nutmeg
1/2 cup white sugar
1/2 tsp. salt
1/2 cup raisins
Cinnamon

Serves 4. Put the rice, milk, cream or top milk, and salt into a greased baking dish. Sprinkle lightly with nutmeg and cinnamon. Bake in oven at 350° for 45 minutes. Stir, add sugar, vanilla, and raisins, and return to oven for 35 minutes, or until milk has cooked into the rice. Stir occasionally. Putting a few marshmallows on top makes an easy meringue. Allow to melt and brown lightly. Serve with mugs of cold milk or hot chocolate, and cookies, for a complete, nutritious meal, much appreciated by children.

RICE TOPPED with SPICY CABBAGE

3 pork chops, large
6 cups green cabbage, shredded
2 tsps. salt
1/4 tsp. each pepper and chili powder
1 cup onions, chopped
1 No. 2 can tomatoes
1/2 cup canned mushrooms, sliced
3 cups hot, cooked rice
1 pimiento, canned

Serves 8. Brown chops in skillet. Enough fat should cook out of the meat so that it is unnecessary to add fat to the skillet. Cut meat into half-inch squares, discard bones. To the meat and fat add onions and some juice from tomatoes. Cover and cook over medium heat until meat is done. Add tomatoes, cabbage, mushrooms, salt, pepper, and chili powder. Cover skillet and cook only until cabbage is tender, but still crisp and green. Add very small amount of water if necessary. Spread hot, cooked rice on heated platter. Serve meat-cabbage mixture over the rice. Decorate with strips of canned pimiento. Deviled hard-boiled eggs are an ideal accompaniment for this luncheon or supper dish.

RICE-STUFFED SQUASH

Stuff boiled halves of acorn squash with a mixture of cooked rice, chopped cooked ham or sausage, grated onion, Tabasco, and soy sauce. Add condensed cream of mushroom soup to make a thick, creamy consistency. Top squash-filling with buttered bread crumbs. Bake until piping hot over hot water. Pass a hot cheese sauce at the table. For this, melt brick cheese in double boiler, adding one-fourth as much bottled mayonnaise as cheese. Season with mustard.

ARROZ con SARDINAS a la CARMEN or RICE with SARDINES

1 onion, chopped
1 can tomato sauce
Sliced ripe olives
Chopped parsley
Lemon wedges
2 tbsps. bacon grease
2 cups raw rice
1 can green peas
2 cans large sardines in tomato sauce
Salt

Serves 4–6. Sauté the onion in the bacon grease. Add the tomato sauce with 2 cups of water, bring to a brisk boil. To this, add 2 tsps. salt and the raw white rice, let come to a boil again, cover, and turn flame low. When rice is dry and steamed, add 1 can peas, drained, and the whole sardines with their tomato sauce. Do not mash sardines but place them carefully on top of rice and peas. Decorate with sliced ripe olives, parsley, and lemon wedges. Serve in same earthenware casserole in which it was cooked on top of stove. This is a purely Monterey version of Arroz con Pollo.

MEAT and RICE CASSEROLE, CARMEL

1 lb. each ground veal and pork
1 onion, sliced
2 (8 oz) cans tomato sauce
1 cup pitted ripe olives
2 cups cooked white rice
1/2 cup Burgundy or claret wine
1/2 cup grated Parmesan cheese
1/2 tsp. sugar
Salt, garlic salt, pepper to taste
Pinch each sweet basil and rosemary
2 tsps. A-1 sauce
3 tbsps. salad oil
Flour

Serves 6. Heat oil in large, heavy skillet, add ground veal and pork, and sliced onion. Cook and stir until meat is no longer pink. Sprinkle flour over meat and onion, blend well. Add tomato sauce and California Burgundy or claret. Cook, stirring until mixture thickens. Add seasoning and cheese, stir over low heat until melted. Combine rice, olives, and meat mixture. Turn into greased casserole. Sprinkle extra grated Parmesan over top. Cover and bake in a moderate oven 30 minutes, uncover and bake 15 minutes longer. Pear and lime-gelatine salad-mold makes a nice combination with this casserole.

THURSDAY NIGHT BEEF STEW with RICE

Serves 6–8. Another California favorite is chuck roast of beef (5 lbs.), marinated for twenty-four hours in 2 cups red table-wine. Add a pinch each of basil, thyme, orégano, rosemary, sliced garlic and onion, lemon slices, whole cloves, and crumbled bayleaf. Brown meat on all sides in vegetable oil. Drain off oil and add to marinade. Cook the pot roast slowly in covered Dutch oven, or pressure cook it according to directions. A short time before serving, add peeled, whole, baby carrots, small pearl onions, and frenched fresh or frozen stringbeans. Remove meat, cut into good-sized squares, add marinade, and heat. Cook down the liquid and serve this glorified stew on top of flaky, white or brown rice. A big bowl of crisp greens—Bibb lettuce, chicory, endive, raw spinach, and thinly sliced Chinese cabbage—dressed with olive oil and wine-herb vinegar, freshly grated peppercorns, garlic salt, and freshly grated Parmesan cheese, will give a true California touch. Red wine, a good, robust California claret or Burgundy, will add the final fillip which makes this meal an especially exciting "Thursday Night" affair—maid's night out or not.

■

Because of the Spanish traditions persisting in California, Spanish Rice is a long-time favorite, and it has endless variations. Either use the canned variety, or concoct your own by mixing sautéed tomatoes, chopped green peppers, and minced onions with cooked rice. Season with orégano, salt, and a little olive oil. Line a casserole with the Spanish rice and top with sautéed, seasoned, ground round of beef, and frozen French-fried onion rings. Heat through in oven. Grated sharp cheese makes a snappy topping, especially when it is decorated with ripe olive half-moons. A fine way to overcome before-payday blues.

IMAGINATIVE CHICKEN and RICE

1 cup diced onion
1 cup diced celery
1 cup peeled apples, diced
2 cups cubed, cooked chicken
1/4 tsp. each rosemary, basil, parsley
1 tbsp. chutney
1/2 tsp. powdered ginger
Salt and pepper
1/2 cup California sherry
1 can condensed cream of mushroom soup
1 small can sliced mushrooms with juice

Serves 6. Cook the onion, celery, and apples gently in butter until soft. Add the next five ingredients and put all together in a buttered casserole. Add the sherry, mushroom soup, and mushrooms with their juice. Blend and bake at 325° until bubbly and golden on top. Serve over dry, flaky, cooked white rice. This is quick and easy, yet imaginative. French garlic bread, using olive oil instead of butter, heated until crisp, is delicious. Cleaned, cooked shrimp, prawn, crayfish, or lobster-tail meat may be used instead of chicken. Always serve over rice. Canned chicken or shrimp and packaged converted or minute rice will speed preparation.

LIGHTNING RICE DISH

Serves 4. Add 1 can condensed cream of celery, chicken, or mushroom soup, diluted with 1 can milk or water, to 2 cups cooked white rice. Add 1 finely chopped, grated, or scraped carrot, 1 package thawed frozen peas, and 1 large can tomatoes minus juice. Season with orégano, thyme, and chopped parsley, onion and garlic juice, salt, pepper, paprika to taste. Simmer, covered, until rice is almost cooked, then add 2 cups leftover cut-up chicken or meat. Put into greased casserole and cook in moderate oven until peas are tender. This dish may be prepared the day before and cooked at the proper time.

■

ITALIAN RICE, MONTEREY

1 lb. prawns or jumbo shrimp
Chopped parsley
Salt, pepper, saffron
1 lb. rice, white or brown
1 clove garlic, minced
Olive oil
Grated Parmesan cheese

Serves 6. Boil the frozen or fresh prawn in salted, seasoned water (add pickling spice, chopped onions, Tabasco sauce to taste) for 10 minutes. Remove and drain. Save the liquid and boil shells from shrimp in it to make a rich broth. In a heavy, Dutch-oven-type pan, put 2 tbsps. olive oil, the minced garlic, and raw rice, adding it gradually. Add more oil if necessary, and stir rice over low fire until oil has been absorbed. Then add the boiling shrimp liquid, strained, a little at a time, stirring continually. After 25 minutes, add whole, cleaned shrimp, chopped parsley, saffron, salt, pepper, and grated Parmesan cheese. The amount of shrimp liquor should be 5 cups liquid to 3 cups rice. It should be absorbed when rice is finished. Place on hot platter, with more freshly grated Parmesan cheese on top. Serve immediately. Sauteéd fresh (or canned) sliced mushrooms may also be added. This recipe was given me by an Italian fisherman's family in Monterey, California. I have lived for many years in nearby Carmel. They served the steaming rice (called risotto in Italian) with roasted, sliced, green peppers and eggplant (unpeeled, dressed with an olive-oil and wine-vinegar sauce). Chianti flowed freely, and crusty rolls were unbuttered but very crisp.

■

CREAMED RICE and MUSSELS

16 fresh or canned mussels
Juice of 1/2 lemon
1 cup white wine
1/2 cup white rice, cooked
3 tbsps. white wine
2 tbsps. butter
1/2 cup mushrooms
Grated nutmeg
1/2 cup top-milk
Seasonings

Serves 4. If you use fresh mussels, be sure there is no ban on them. When cooking fresh ones, wash the shells thoroughly and steam them in small amount of water until shells open. Drain, remove shells and the horny "beard." Put them in saucepan with salt, pepper, Tabasco to taste, and 3 tbsps. white wine. Simmer gently 5 minutes. Add the melted butter, sliced fresh or canned mushrooms, lemon juice, top milk, nutmeg, and dry California white wine. Cook and stir until it thickens a bit, then add the cooked rice. Keep hot in chafing dish. This same dish is excellent made with a combination of shrimp, lobster, oysters, or crab meat.

DEL MONTE CHICKEN with RICE

1 fowl, 5 to 6 lbs.
2 cups California sauterne
2 cups water
2 tsps. salt
1/4 tsp. pepper
1/4 tsp. tarragon
2 tbsps. chopped parsley
1 canned pimiento, minced
12 small onions
12 dried prunes
1 (6 oz.) can whole mushrooms with juice (or 1/4 lb. small fresh mushrooms)
1/2 cup flour
1/2 cup water
2 cups cooked rice

Serves 6. Disjoint and cut up fowl. Mix wine and water together in large Dutch oven. Bring to a boil and add chicken and seasonings, excepting pimiento. Simmer until chicken is tender. Time will be shortened by using pressure cooker according to directions, or use 2 whole canned chickens, meat removed from bones in good-sized serving pieces. To the chicken liquid, add vegetables and prunes. Boil in stock until tender and liquid is reduced to 4 cups. Mix flour and water together until smooth, pour mixture into liquid, stir until thickened. Place chicken slices in 2-qt. casserole. Cover with gravy, vegetables, and prunes. Top with cooked, hot rice; dot with butter; and sprinkle with pimiento. Heat through in oven until bubbly and the rice-topping is golden brown. Serve with garlic-flavored, tossed, green salad and crisp, warm cheese straws. Chilled California sauterne and demitasses complete this de luxe, but easily prepared, one-dish meal.

VEAL with RICE RING

2 lbs. veal round steak
1 onion, chopped
1 can consommé
1 cup sour cream
1/2 cup shredded Gruyère cheese
Salt, pepper, paprika
Pinch each of thyme and marjoram
Chopped chives
1 cup Rhine wine
4 tbsps. bacon grease
5 tbsps. flour
1 (4 oz.) can sliced mushrooms, and juice
1/2 tsp. Worcestershire sauce
2 tsps. lemon juice
1 tsp. grated lemon rind
4 cups cooked rice

Serves 6. Heat bacon drippings in a large, heavy skillet with a tight fitting lid,; add veal, cut into 1½ inch cubes, and onion. Cook, stirring frequently, until meat is nicely browned. Sprinkle flour over veal and onion, stir until pieces of meat are coated with the flour. Add consommé and California Rhine-type wine; cook and stir until gravy is thickened and smooth; add mushrooms with liquid and seasonings. Cover and simmer gently 45 minutes, stirring often. Add a little more wine if mixture evaporates. It should be fairly thick when served. Then add the shredded Gruyère-type cheese and the sour cream. Simmer until cheese is melted. Pack the rice into a buttered ring mold and steam a few minutes. Unmold and fill center with creamed veal. It tastes best when glasses of well-chilled California Rhine wine are served with this delicious one-plate meal. Crusty rolls may be included.

SHERRIED BEEF MUFFINS con ARROZ

1 lb. ground beef
1 egg
2 tbsps. minced onion
1/2 can condensed cream of mushroom soup
1/2 cup dry California sherry
1 cup cooked white rice

Serves 4. Mix ingredients together. Add salt and pepper to taste. Grease large muffin tins and fill with mixture. Bake in moderate oven for 45 minutes. Remove from tins by turning upside down on platter. Serve with following sauce:

2 tbsps. butter
1 can condensed mushroom soup
Salt, pepper, cayenne
1/2 cup dry California sherry
1 cup milk
3 tbsps. flour
1 tsp. Worcestershire sauce

Melt butter and stir in flour, add cream of mushroom soup and milk; cook, stirring until mixture thickens. Add remaining ingredients. Serve piping hot. This is a good sauce for any meat, poultry, or seafood served over flaky rice. Raw, crisp vegetables are all that is needed with these unusual muffins. A glass of wine, or two, is a delightful way to say: "¡Qué bueno!"

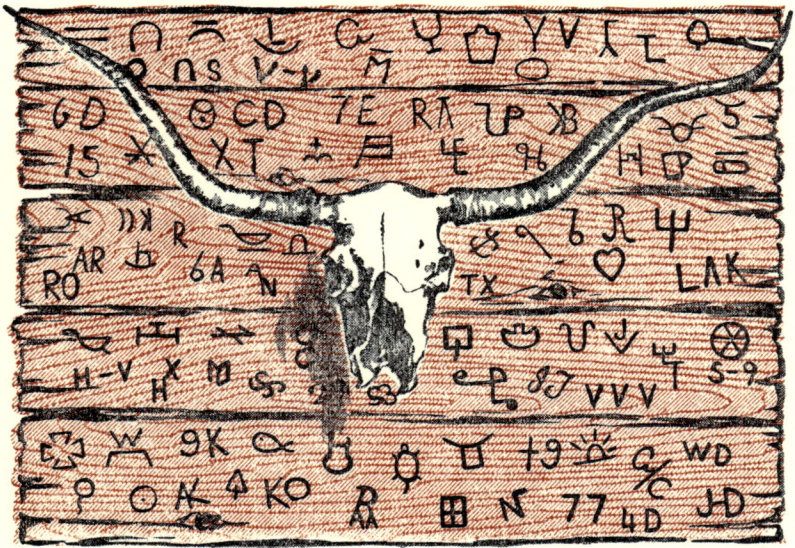

TEXAS TASTE

■■■When we were stationed with the U.S. Cavalry on the Texas border, we had the most marvelous food in existence and matching appetites! Riding horseback instead of walking, we always wore riding breeches and boots—excepting when the gals switched to evening dresses. There were wonderful fresh fruits growing in our back yards. The vegetables, fresh meats, and wild game birds were plentiful and terribly cheap. Our husbands shot wild ducks and "white wings" (doves) almost daily, as hunting was open season on the Mexican side of the border. We loved the savory chili always served over flaky rice in great quantity. The following recipes are those which my Mexican cook, Concha, concocted with a special flair of her own.

One of our menus for visiting V.I.P.'s was the following:

Cantaloupe with Jellied Madrilène
Cheese Straws
Country Captain   Onions de Luxe
Sherried Pink Grapefruit

■

COUNTRY CAPTAIN

4 frying chickens, cut up
Seasoned flour
Shortening
Cooked white rice
3 onions, chopped
2 cloves garlic, minced
1 cup almonds, blanched
1 large can mushrooms
2 green peppers, chopped
2 large cans tomatoes
1 cup raisins or currants, soaked and drained
Chopped parsley

Serves 8. Shake the chicken in paper bag containing flour, chili powder, salt, pepper, thyme, paprika. Be sure each piece is well coated. Fry in shortening or bacon drippings, until light brown on both sides and cooked thoroughly, yet juicy.

Make a sauce of the remaining ingredients, except rice. Sauté onions, green pepper, and garlic in the fat in which chickens were browned, adding more if necessary. Add tomatoes, whole almonds, currants or raisins, and fresh or canned mushrooms. Arrange chicken in layers in large baking dish with sauce in between layers. Finish off with the sauce. Save some almonds, raisins, and the parsley, with which to decorate top. Heat through in oven. This dish is very pretty if chicken and sauce are put in center of large, round platter with the hot white rice surrounding it. Pass extra sauce at the table. Some Texans use curry powder, instead of chili powder, but the latter seems more Texan to me. The above amount serves generous portions, with seconds always received enthusiastically.

■

TEXAS ONIONS de LUXE

Serves 6. This is a perfect team-mate for Texas-inspired dishes. Slice 2 sweet Texas (or Bermuda) onions into thin rings. Add 1 cucumber, thinly sliced, leaving half of green rind, when peeling, to add cool color. Run the prongs of a silver fork down length of cucumber and rind. This gives a scalloped effect to the rings. Combine with a few unpeeled, sliced, red radishes. Season with dill, salt, and paprika. Mix with 1 pint commercial sour cream to which 2 tsps. fresh lemon juice is added. Mix lightly, serve icy cold in glass bowl. Men go for this with zest. In the wide, open spaces, no one cares if they smell "onion-ey" or not! This smooth salad-relish blends with highly spiced Texas specialties. Cold beer is another necessity, one might say. The blandness of piping hot rice also counteracts the sometimes fiery chili dishes. Rice is extensively grown in Texas and Arkansas.

SIMPLE CHILI and RICE

Serves 4. **In contrast to the partified Country Captain, this everyday dish is simplicity itself. Merely empty** contents of 1 can best chili con carne, with beans, into a Mexican earthenware baking dish. Add 1 can tomato purée. Sprinkle finely chopped, raw onion over top. Heat through in oven. Onion does not have to cook. In fact, onions are often served in a separate side-dish at table to be added at one's own discretion. Serve over boiled white rice, dry and flaky. I use converted rice, which is processed in Texas, and what a time-saver it is! One is always sure of **perfect results, which is the main object in rice cookery.**

■

FEATHERED RICE

1 cup rice, long grain
2 cups chicken broth or any preferred liquid
1 clove garlic, mashed

Serves 2–3. Put the long-grain, raw white rice on a shallow baking sheet. Brown in a 375° oven, watching and stirring with a long-handled fork. When browned, remove and put in earthenware saucepan. Add the boiling chicken broth, tomato or vegetable juice, consommé, soup stock (clam juice for seafood dishes), or plain water, if preferred. Salt to taste, and distribute the mashed garlic (or use a garlic press to get the juice) evenly throughout the rice. Bake in a 350° oven for 30 minutes. This is the base for the addition of cubed, cooked meats, shellfish, fish, ham, game, hard-cooked eggs, and/or cheese. Pretty, dark-eyed Concha, with her flashing smile, taught me to prepare this feathered rice.

There seemed to be no end to the variety of one-dish meals she could produce, starting with the rice as a base. We often use packaged brown rice as a change from the white. Brown rice is nutty in flavor. It is the whole, unpolished grain of rice with only the outer, inedible fibrous hull removed. In its natural state, all its original salts and vitamins are retained. Directions are on package. Children love it, with cut-up, cooked dried fruits added, as a cereal for breakfast.

TEXAS-STYLE MEXICAN RICE

Serves 6. Here is another simple supper dish. In an earthenware casserole, on top of stove, put 1 cup olive oil. Lightly sauté 2 cups raw rice until evenly gold-hued, stirring frequently. Add 1 chopped onion and 1 minced garlic clove with ½ green pepper, chopped. Stir to keep from burning. Add 2 cups tomato or vegetable juice, 2 cups undiluted canned consommé. Season to taste with celery salt, paprika, cayenne, and a pinch of fresh chili powder. Bring to a brisk boil, then reduce at once to a very low fire. Put casserole over asbestos mat. Keep lid on tightly. Cook about 30 minutes without lifting lid. If converted or minute rice is used, cook according to directions on packages. Liquid should be absorbed, and rice dry and crisp. You may add cut-up fried bacon, ham, salt pork, sausage meat, or ground round of beef, in the quantity you prefer.

Serve with avocados-on-the-half-shell, sprinkled with salt and fresh lime juice. A "Shandygaff" is a fine drink to soothe the most parched of throats, after riding in the Texas sand-dust-sun on that favorite hunter of yours. A "Shandygaff" is half stout and half gingerale...icy cold.

RICE RING RIO GRANDE

6 frankfurters
1 lb. ground round of beef
Butter
2 onions, chopped
1/2 green pepper, chopped
Salt, pepper, chili powder, paprika
1 can tomato paste
Parmesan cheese
1 clove garlic, minced
1 cup consommé
1 pkg. frozen peas
2 cups cooked brown or white rice
Canned pimiento

Serves 6–8. Cut frankfurters in rings and sauté in butter. Remove, and in same pan sauté the onions, minced garlic, and green pepper. Add the ground round of beef and brown. Add tomato paste, seasonings, and consommé. When heated through, add the cooked rice, mix lightly with fork. Cook the frozen peas quickly until bright green. Drain. Fresh chopped mint and sugar, added to the peas, with butter, improve their flavor. Oil a ring mold, decorate bottom with sliced frankfurters, putting little heaps of lovely green peas in between. Add rice mixture and keep over boiling water. Remove onto a round, hot platter. Sprinkle grated Parmesan cheese over all. Garnish with pimiento, more peas, and frankfurters. This may be prepared the day before, and reheated by putting mold covered with wax paper or foil over boiling water.

Cold beer in tall, thin, blue or green Mexican glasses, and Texas pink grapefruit, broiled with sherry or bourbon, climax one of our favorite meals.

1 lb. ground beef
1 clove garlic, minced
1 tbsp. chili powder
Salt and pepper
1/2 green pepper, chopped
1 onion, chopped
1 white potato, diced
Dry white rice

CONCHA'S STEW or STEAMBOAT HASH

Serves 4. Brown beef in bacon fat, add other ingredients, cover with water, but do not "drown." Simmer until onion, green pepper, garlic, and potato are done. Serve over hot, buttered rice. Include steaming, buttered cornbread and a green salad of young, tender spinach leaves with pink grapefruit sections topped with cottage cheese.

The "Steamboat Hash," as the original Galveston recipe is called, became a great family favorite and was renamed "Concha's Stew" by our young son. He and his friends preferred it to anything else. When not in school or asleep, they were either riding horseback or merrily filling themselves with Conchita's good stew.

LOUISIANA'S JAMBALAYA

■ ■ ■ One of my warm friends, born in Louisiana, tells me that her nightly prayer as a child in New Orleans was always the same: "God bless pahpah and mahmah and rice and gravy."

From this same reliable source, the witty and penetrating Mrs. McNeese, whose book reviews are so famous in Washington, I learned that the rice grown "back when" (before modern irrigation methods were used) was called "Providence" rice. They had to depend upon the elements in those early times for the necessary moisture rice raising demands. "Providence" rice seems a most fitting appellation as today Louisiana is the largest rice-growing state in our country, although Arkansas, Texas, and California are strong competitors. These states are exporting rice today.

Rice plantations date from 1718 in Louisiana but it was not until after the Civil War in 1864 that this state's planters saw rice culture become the surely providential success it is now. While the Low Country of South Carolina was the birthplace of rice in America, its initial prosperity declined after the War Between the States.

■

1 medium can tomato sauce
Leaves of 3 stalks celery
1 small green pepper
2 cloves garlic
2 small onions
2 lbs. raw, peeled crayfish (écrivisses)
3 cups cooked white rice
Dash of cayenne
Salt and pepper

JAMBALAYA aux ÉCRIVISSES à la LOUISIANE

Serves 8. Brown onion, pepper, garlic, and celery leaves, all chopped, in olive oil in a deep saucepan. Add tomato sauce and seasonings. Simmer on low heat to make a purée. After ½ hour, add crayfish and boil about 15 minutes. Add cooked rice when crayfish are about half-done. Cubed, cooked ham may be added. Serve with red wine and garlic French bread.

Jumbo shrimp may be substituted for the écrivisses.

This and the following recipe are treasured family heirlooms of Alice Sullivan O'Keefe, native Louisianian.

JAMBALAYA LAFITTE

- 1 lb. raw ham
- 1 tbsp. bacon fat
- 1 cup peeled, chopped tomatoes
- 1/2 lb. breakfast sausage
- 1/2 cup chopped onions
- 1 clove garlic, mashed
- 1/2 pod red pepper or 1 tsp. "pepperoni"
- 1 tbsp. flour
- 1 lb. raw shrimp
- 1 doz. oysters
- 2 cups canned consommé
- 2 tbsps. chopped parsley
- 1 cup uncooked rice
- Salt, pepper, paprika, thyme

Serves 6. Heat bacon fat in heavy pot. Add onions, brown lightly; add flour and brown. Add ham cut into small pieces; skinned sausages; washed, shelled, raw shrimp; and tomatoes. Simmer covered for ½ hour. Add garlic, the red pepper, parsley, rice, consommé, and the seasonings. Cook covered until rice is done but not gummy. Add oysters, cooking 2 minutes. Serve from heated casserole or chafing dish at table. A simple salad and garlic-toasted bread make the meal complete. The highly seasoned raciness of this dish is reminiscent of the derring-do of the French buccaneer Lafitte, who operated in this same Gulf of Mexico area.

Strong Louisiana coffee always on hand tastes good. If the occasion is festive, "Café Brulot" will add glamour. Café Brulot is made by putting very thin orange and lemon rinds in a chafing dish with some whole allspice and a stick of cinnamon. Add three lumps of sugar soaked in best brandy. Heat some extra brandy in a ladle, then light it in the chafing dish until the sugar dissolves. Add freshly made, strong, Louisiana coffee, about 3 large cups. Serve in demitasses. This is more dramatic if it takes place in a darkened dining or living room. Even though this Louisiana ceremony is intended to be performed with a flourish, be careful not to lean over the brandy while it is burning— it may singe off your eyebrows, which happened to our host.

What a surprise to find his eyebrows gone in a matter of seconds!

■

2 cups raw rice
2 thin slices ham, smoked
1 qt. fresh milk
Mustard, paprika, Onion juice

ESCALLOPED RICE and HAM

Serves 6. Place a layer of rice in 2 qt. casserole. Place on this a slice of ham, cut into servings, then more rice, then another slice of ham, then top with rice. The seasonings are sprinkled on the ham. Pour on the tepid milk. Bake in a moderate oven one hour or longer, until rice is cooked but not mushy. This is fine for brunch on Sunday.

■

3 cups boiled rice
1 sweet red pepper
1 onion
1 lb. sausages
1 cup milk
Butter

SURPRISE RICE

Serves 6. Remove seeds from sweet red pepper, chop and parboil pepper. Add it with finely chopped onion to butter and brown lightly. Mix this into cooked rice carefully. Put a layer of this mixture in a buttered baking dish, add a layer of cooked sausage, and cover with rice. Pour milk over all and dot with butter. Bake until bubbly and light brown. Serve for breakfast on Sunday with cups of steaming New Orleans coffee and sweet rolls.

KENTUCKY'S BURGOO

■■■ My father, who was born at the old family plantation outside of Louisville, often told me of his boyhood there. In those times, during the short days of the winter, "lamplighter hours" were spent by a glowing fireplace. Here supper was cooked in old black pots suspended from cranes or pot hooks. A sturdy Kentucky Burgoo and steaming white rice were dished out from the pots, and the evening meal took place around the hearthside.

Similar to the famous Virginia Brunswick Stew, Kentucky's traditional dish is enhanced with the addition of flaky white rice. If you do not own a "black pot complete with crane" (and most of us do not), simmer this authentic "receipt" of my family's in a Dutch oven on the kitchen stove. Bring the pot, and another pot of rice, to the fireplace hearth and serve the burgoo in pottery bowls on individual trays. Have a blazing fire so that no other lights are used. Sit about on cushions or footstools to sip this savory stew, a meal in itself if there ever was one. This heart-warming, thick stew may be transferred to an outdoor barbecue setting, weather permitting. Incidentally, this is a fine way to entertain at a "Firelit Potluck Supper."

Squirrels were originally the basis of this open-air stew, but nowadays chicken and meat are used for the firelit version.

KENTUCKY BURGOO with RICE

1 5-lb. hen
1 lb. ground beef
6 thick slices bacon
1 cup butter (lima) beans
1 cup stringbeans
1 cup okra
6 tomatoes, cut up
1 cup diced onions
2 white potatoes, diced
Salt, pepper, Tabasco sauce
Lemon juice
Sugar
Fresh, scraped, green corn
Nutmeg, butter
Hot white rice

Serves 12. Simmer the chicken in seasoned, boiling water in an iron pot or Dutch oven until tender. Dice chicken, discarding bones. Return to pot with broth and add all ingredients except corn, nutmeg, and butter. There should always be enough liquid to cover vegetables while cooking. I substitute frozen vegetables for the fresh ones in the original "receipt." Stir often with long-handled spoon. Add the corn toward the end. When mixture begins to thicken, but is still "soupy," add grated nutmeg and butter. Serve very hot over steaming white rice.

SOUTH CAROLINA'S GOLD

■■■ Charleston is a charming old Southern city. So replete is it with memories of plantation days that during our many visits there we felt we had been transported to another era.

For us two significant facts stand out: (1) Charleston was the birthplace of rice in America. (2) My husband's ancestor was among the first to receive and plant the rice.

The rice arrived there quite by accident. In 1694, a brigantine built in New England, but en route from Madagascar, put into Charles Towne harbor in distress. To return the kindness of a few of the leading English colonists, the ship's master distributed a packet of unhusked rice amongst them. One of these was Landgrave Thomas Smith, from whom my husband is directly descended. The Landgrave, who was governor of Carolina at the time, planted some of the rice in his own garden patch. From the rough rice grew the seeds of prosperity. Rice plantations flourished and so did the Colony. Within a small number of years, this lucky grain from Madagascar was named "Carolina Golden Rice." Since that time rice has been one of the favorite foods of the South and is becoming increasingly so throughout the whole United States.

RICE GRIDDLE CAKES

1 cup cold cooked rice
1/4 cup milk and additional milk
1 tsp. melted butter
1 egg, separated
1 tsp. sugar
1/4 tsp. salt
1 tsp. baking powder
1/2 cup flour

Serves 3. Steam the rice in ¼ cup milk until soft. Add enough milk to make ¾ cup in all. Mix in butter, beaten egg yolk, sugar, salt, and flour sifted with baking powder. Fold in egg white, beaten stiff. Bake on greased griddle iron. Serve with currant jelly for breakfast.

RICE PIE

Serves 4. Red Rice is one of the more customary dishes in this part of the South. It is prepared by cooking 1 cup raw Carolina rice with a ham bone with meat on it and simmering both in just enough water to cover. Add 2 cut-up fresh tomatoes. Season to taste. Cook gently with cover tightly on until rice is dry. Remove ham bone, add minced ham. Excellent with roast chicken or game.

CASSEROLE of HOPPIN' JOHN

2 cups blackeyed peas
1 ham hock
Piece of fat from salt pork
2 cups raw Carolina rice
2 onions, sliced
1 green pepper, chopped
Salt, pepper, red pepper
1 canned pimiento
Tabasco sauce

Serves 12. Soak the blackeyed peas overnight. In South Carolina, they use cowpeas, known as dried field peas, or small brown peas. As they are not a familiar item in the North, use blackeyed peas. The scrubbed ham hock should be quite meaty. The "roots" of a boiled smoked tongue will also add flavor. Include some "fat back," or a piece of fat from salt pork. Soak these with the blackeyed peas. Next day, do not change water as it is full of rich nuances. Boil gently until peas and ham are tender, then remove ham and cut into medium pieces, return to peas and liquid. Sauté the onions and green pepper. Add these and rice to peas and ham. There should be 4 cups liquid in which to cook rice. Cover and cook rapidly at first, then steam for 20 minutes. Liquid should be almost entirely absorbed. Season with salt, pepper, a few drops of Tabasco, or the native-grown, powdered, red pepper. Do not make really "hot" to the palate, just a suspicion to spark the blandness. Put in large, heated casserole or chafing dish. Decorate with thin slices of canned pimiento. Serve with boiled turnip greens (I use frozen chopped collards). Pass a cruet of vinegar with these. Piping hot corn bread or batter bread completes a heart-warming meal.

Always on New Year's Day, "Hoppin' John" is served

in the most stately mansions and eaten in the smallest cabins in South Carolina. This custom is said to bring good luck for the rest of the year. It is also eaten with gusto by many every day. An economical dish, it is easily prepared and is very savory and nutritious.

SPECIAL BATTER BREAD

4 fresh eggs
1½ tsps. salt
Butter
3/4 cup waterground cornmeal
3 tsps. baking powder
1 qt. fresh milk

Serves 8. Beat the eggs, add cornmeal and baking powder mixed together with salt. Mix throughly. Add slowly the milk, which has stood at room temperature until tepid. Stir again until smooth. Pour into two buttered Pyrex loaf pans. Bake in preheated 350° oven 30 minutes on lower shelf. Serve hot with butter and a pitcher of corn syrup.

This "receipt" is over 300 years old and is treasured as a family heirloom. It is infallible and "unfallable," so prepare a lot. It will disappear as fast as the proverbial Northern hot cakes.

In the days when Charleston was a great seaport, before the Revolutionary War, many ships from the Orient arrived with ideas which were adapted to the Carolina-grown produce. Rice being the reigning commodity, the Carolinians copied Oriental "pilaffs" for their own pilaus, pronounced "pélos." They are favorite dishes today and make splendid one-dish fare.

PILAU of SEAFOOD

1 onion, chopped
2 tbsps. butter
1 cup tomatoes
1/2 tsp. salt
1/2 tsp. paprika
1 cup raw Carolina rice
1 cup clam juice
1 cup vegetable juice
1 bayleaf, crumbled
1 cup cooked shrimp or crab meat

Serves 6. Cook onion in butter until golden. Stir in rice until lightly colored. Add clam and vegetable juices, tomatoes, bayleaf, salt, and paprika (or powdered red pepper) to taste. Fold in seafood, with a little cut-up boiled ham if desired. Cover the skillet and bring to boil, then reduce heat to simmer for 25 minutes, or until rice is right consistency. Cut-up young, fresh (or frozen) okra may also be added. This pilau may be baked in a greased casserole and served at the table from same dish.

Hot biscuits and preserves with chilled sauterne makes this an enviable repast.

Since the early days when the Carolina Lowlands grew wealthy on vast rice plantations, this nourishing cereal has been a most popular food. Combined in these interesting dishes, rice has always proven delectable and satisfying. The cracked variety was used at first, it being less expensive and sweeter than the polished whole grain.

CHICKEN PILAU

Bacon drippings
1 tbsp. chopped parsley
4 slices bacon
1 No. 2½ can tomatoes
1 tbsp. chopped green pepper
1 onion, cut up
1 cup okra
1 tbsp. sugar
1 tsp. salt
1/2 cup water
Pepper, powdered red pepper
2 cups cubed, cooked chicken
1 cup raw Carolina rice

Serves 6. Dice bacon and fry in skillet until crisp. Drain on absorbent paper. Cook onion and green pepper in bacon drippings until limp. Add canned tomatoes, uncooked rice, thinly sliced okra, water, salt, sugar, black pepper, red pepper, and the chicken. Cover closely and simmer for 20 minutes, or until rice is tender. Just before serving, add crisp bacon and chopped parsley. This may be cooked in a moderate oven or on top of stove.

A pilau may be varied by adding more or less okra or tomato and leaving out the chicken. Then it becomes simply Tomato or Okra Pilau. A quaint title for an Okra Pilau is "Limping Susan," named after the cook, no doubt. The foundation of all pilaus is rice, and a very grand dish it makes.

RED RICE

Serves 6. Mix into 2 cups boiled rice, 2 tbsps. melted butter, and 1 beaten egg. Line a deep dish with this. Have ready a nicely seasoned stew of beef or any meat and 2 sliced, cooked eggs. Put these into the rice-lined baking dish, cover with the remaining rice, dot with butter and chopped parsley, and bake until bubbly and light brown.

SHRIMP and EGGPLANT PIE

1 cup cooked shrimp
1 egg, beaten
1 eggplant, cubed
Salt, pepper, thyme
1 cup cooked rice
1 tsp. Worcestershire sauce
2 tbsps. melted butter
1 onion, minced

Serves 4-6. Sauté onion in butter, add to shrimp, rice, and the cooked cubes of eggplant (parboil quickly in boiling, salted water, drain). Season all with Worcestershire, salt, pepper, and powdered thyme. Mix together and bake in buttered casserole in moderate oven for 30 minutes. Grated Parmesan cheese makes a nice topping. Serve with hot biscuits and watermelon pickles.

GUMBO SOUP

2 lbs. round of beef or chicken
1 onion, chopped
2 doz. okras, sliced
1 green pepper, chopped
3 stalks of celery, diced
Cooked ham
2 cups canned tomatoes
Seasonings to taste
Cubes of bacon or salt pork
Herbs to taste

Serves 6. Cut beef or chicken in good-sized pieces and brown in butter with the onion. Add okra, pepper, and celery. Add bacon or salt pork, and fry together. Put everything in deep saucepan, add cut-up, cooked ham, and tomatoes, and season to taste. Herbs are always used sparingly but are an asset. Cover with boiling water and cook very slowly for about 2 hours. Skim off fat. This gumbo may also be prepared with crabmeat or fresh shrimp. Always pass a big, covered dish of boiled rice, very dry and flaky. Serve gumbo from tureen into deep soup plates, adding rice as desired.

While gumbos are usually associated with Louisiana, they are also greatly used in South Carolina. The above "receipt" is a meal in itself. The beauty of it is that any leftover gumbo may be kept in sealed glass jars in the refrigerator for days.

WASHINGTON WHIRL

■■■ International cuisine is a specialty of Washington's party-going crowd. Each embassy features its own gastronomy par excellence. At the lavish receptions, these foreign dishes take top billing on the menu. Interest is so widespread that International Cooking courses are given at the YWCA. One of the most popular of the series is the favorite dishes of the Middle East. The typical Arabic "Fetteh and Rice" is concocted of lamb shanks, rice, and vegetables, steamed until tender, then combined with browned pine nuts and broth in "community bowls." Arab protocol decides which people in the group invited will dine from the bowl first. Even though the rice is hot, each person scoops it up with his hand, rolls the rice in his fingers to form a ball, and eats it, dipped in spicy sauce. This is not done at receptions in Washington, however.

Arabic Rice is cooked by adding cinnamon, nutmeg, and allspice to the boiling, salted water (2 cups water to 1 cup rice). It is delicious with Shish Kebab. We have read that the sheiks serve "an imperial 'kousy,'" a dish larger than most table tops, filled with a mountain of rice and topped with two whole roast young lambs, meltingly tender under the fingers, with the rich stuffing of spiced rice and raisins and almonds and bits of liver lying all about them." This is the way Joseph Alsop describes this mighty dish in his column. (This quotation was used by permission of the *New York Herald Tribune*.) Often there are seven kinds of rice at these Near East and Middle East parties.

But as my aim is to describe one-dish rice meals suitable for everyday kitchens and tables, I will go on to describe a delectable, but more practical, Cuban rice dish, which I know only too well. I must have cooked it at least thirty-six times at the various Latin American embassies, the Chief of Staff's quarters at Fort Myer, and at the White House!

For some years I was a member of the gay White House Spanish Study Group. To maintain his pupils' interest (they being long since past school age), the professor, an energetic Cuban, prepared a monthly luncheon. The members took turns cooking "á la española," with "el profesór" the presiding chef. I became his chief assistant. These happy fiestas took place at the Latin American embassies, the Army Chief of Staff's quarters, and closed the "school" season at the White House. Both Mrs. Truman and Mrs. Eisenhower were enthusiastic students.

At the White House, eight of us worked hard in the spacious kitchen. The permanent cooking staff stood by while we "cooks for a morning" took over. At one o'clock, our luncheon was served in the State Dining Room. The setting of dark oak panels, crystal chandeliers, and flower-decked tables, each seating six, was most attractive. Lincoln's portrait gazed down as though approving of this modern day Latin American party in the "President's House."

This was our Cuban luncheon as served in the White House:

In Red Room
Jerez Amontillado

In State Dining Room
**Picadillo on Fluffy White Rice
Hot, Buttered, Hard, Crusty Bread
Vino Tinto
Mixed Green Salad, Salsa Ramón
Guava Paste on Bland Cheese
Black Cuban Coffee**

■

SALSA RAMÓN

1 qt. mayonnaise
2 cloves garlic, minced
Salt, paprika
Juice of 2 lemons
3 tbsps. Worcestershire sauce
1/2 tsp. Tabasco sauce
2 tbsp. wine vinegar

Beat the above ingredients together with a rotary beater. Then squeeze the mixture through the same white cloth bag mentioned in Cuban Picadillo. This gives a flavor otherwise unobtainable. This sauce will keep well in a sealed jar in the refrigerator. It is excellent on fish or meats.

The mixed green salad mentioned in the above given menu contained endive, romaine, Boston and Iceberg lettuce, watercress, Bibb lettuce, thin slices of cucumber with the skins left on, firm tomato, radish, celery, and cauliflower slices. It was made quite picante with this spicy dressing.

CUBAN PICADILLO and FLUFFY WHITE RICE

1½ lbs. round beef, 1 lb. lamb, 1/2 lb. pork, ground together
1 cup blanched almonds
1 cup seedless raisins
2 tbsps. crushed Mexican pepper seeds (pepperoni)
2 tsps. saffron powder
3 bay leaves, crumbled
3 hard-cooked eggs
1 small can pimiento
2 sticks butter (1 cup)
6 each large tomatoes and onions, chopped
1 large green pepper, chopped

6 cloves garlic, minced
Juice of 3 lemons
12 large green olives
3 tbsps. capers
3 tbsps. chopped parsley
2 cups California claret
Salt to taste
1 tsp. each powdered cumin seed and orégano
Fluffy white rice

Serves 12. Blend the meat well with fingers. In an iron skillet, lightly sauté the cut-up tomatoes and green pepper, peeled onions, and garlic cloves in half the butter. Put a layer of the mixed meats in the bottom of a big iron pot, or Dutch oven, sprinkle with salt, add several spoons of the tomato mixture, a little lemon juice, some of the blanched almonds, left whole, some of the raisins, a few sliced green olives with juice, a bit of the crushed pepper seeds (called pepperoni). Next add a pinch of saffron powder. Sprinkle some capers, with juice, and chopped parsley, then a good pinch of each of the crumbled bay leaves, powdered cumin seed, and orégano. These three were previously pounded to a fine powder in a white muslin bag. Save the bag to be used later. Now add another layer of the meats and repeat above procedure until all ingredients are used. Pour slowly over all, the claret and enough water to come just to brim of meat mixture. Leave pot uncovered. Simmer slowly over low heat on top of stove for 2 hours. Use long wooden spoon to stir, to prevent scorching. This dish has a fair amount of liquid and is served hot over fluffy rice.

Professor Ramón Ramos, our chef and mentor, often would substitute chicken breasts for the chopped meats in his picadillo. The method of cooking was the same. He always told us that this flavorsome dish would be as lacking as a sandwich without bread if it did not rest sublimely on a nest of lovely, flaky, white rice.

Fluffy White Rice, Cuban Style

Serves 12. Put 2 lbs. washed rice into heavy pot, cover with boiling water, add 1 tbsp. salt. Lower heat. After water comes to a vigorous boil again, cover pot, and steam until grains are tender, testing between fingers. Rinse in large colander until water is clear. Into a separate pot, put ½ stick butter, add drained rice with rest of butter on top. Lay a piece of wet, brown, wrapping paper over rice and put pot in slow oven. When the paper is dry, put rice on top of stove over the lowest heat possible. Each grain should be distinct and separate. To serve, place generous mounds of rice on heated plates, make well in each, fill with hot picadillo and juices. Decorate each portion with thinly sliced, hard-cooked eggs and strips of pimiento.

"¡ Salud y pesetas y tiempo para gustarlos!" "Here's to your good health and wealth, with time in which to enjoy them!"

In the Near East, Turkey, the Balkans, and Greece, pilaff is the main dish. The name of this favorite dish has many spellings: the East-Indian "Pulao," the Turkish and Greek "Pilaff," the Arabian "Pilaw," the Oriental "Pilaf," and the Charleston, S.C. "Pilau" (pronounced pélo). Its basis is fried rice with stock added, tomatoes, onions, other spicy seasonings, and often chopped meats or chicken. The whole is simmered until the moisture is absorbed and the grains of rice are distinct and separate—and oh, so flavor-packed. The following are three choice recipes given me by members of these Near Eastern embassies in Washington.

■

1/2 lb. ground pork
1/2 lb. ground veal or beef
Salt, pepper
1 onion, shredded
1 clove garlic, minced
Parsley, chopped
1 bay leaf
Ground cloves
A few capers
Some dry mustard
Olive oil
Chopped pimiento
A taste of sugar

NEAR EASTERN MEAT BALLS and RICE

Serves 6. Make meat balls, adding the salt, pepper, onions, garlic, and parsley to taste. Roll each in flour. Brown in olive oil on all sides. Put the tomato paste in a separate pan with the bay leaf, crumbled, the cloves, celery, capers, dry mustard, pimiento, and sugar. Season to taste for individual preference. The Near Easterners prefer their dishes spicy and a little sweet. Cook the tomato mixture slowly until

well blended. Press through sieve. Add broth, well seasoned, and a little more tomato paste, if sauce evaporates. Serve meat balls and sauce over hot, cooked rice. Some rice may be added to the meat balls in the making, to bind them.

CHICKEN PILAFF

1 fricassee chicken
1 lb. walnuts, ground
4 onions
1 wineglass sauterne
Juice of 1/2 lemon
Salt, thyme
Sweet red-pepper seeds
Cooked white rice

Serves 6. Cut up the chicken. Steam in covered pot in small amount of water with onions, salt, and crushed pepper seeds. Crush ground walnuts in a mortar with a pestle until slightly oily. Add to fowl after it has steamed for 1 hour. Continue to steam until tender. Add sauterne and lemon juice before serving in a border of cooked white rice.

SYRIAN CHICKEN and RICE

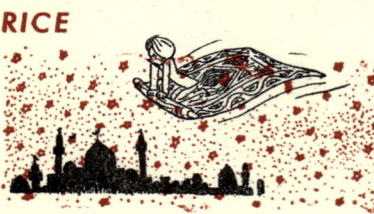

1 lb. rice
1 lb. lamb
1 fat chicken
1 lb. onions
4 cloves garlic
1/4 lb. chick peas
Olive oil
Salt, pepper, paprika
Parsley

Serves 8–10. Brown onions and garlic, each chopped finely, in olive oil. When golden add cut-up meat and chicken and brown. Add soaked chick peas. Season, and cover just to the top with water or broth. Cook slowly for about 2 hours. Add rice during the last 30 minutes, and let dry out.

■

In the Georgetown home of White Russian friends of ours, here in Washington, we often have this delicious menu:.

    Jellied Borscht
   Beef Stroganov on Rice
   Russian Tea Paskha

■

JELLIED BORSCHT

2 cans consommé
1 cup hot water
2 tbsps. unflavored gelatin
2 cups canned shredded beets with juice
Tomato ketchup
Lemon juice
Onion juice
Salt, pepper
Sour cream
Chopped chives or caviar

Serves 6. Soak gelatine in a little lemon and onion juice (about 1 tbsp. each). Add heated consommé and water. Stir until dissolved. Add beets, chopped finely, and enough juice to color a bright red. Put in the ketchup or chili sauce (about 4 tbsps.) and season to taste. Blend well. Chill until very firm. When ready to serve, break up the jellied borscht lightly with a fork. Place in individual glass cups, put 1 tsp. commercial sour cream on each. Add a dash of onion powder, chives, and some red or black caviar, if desired. Chopped, cooked eggplant, mixed with a tart French dressing and served chilled, resembles caviar so well that you can hardly tell it isn't the real thing. This is nice as a topping for the jellied borscht. Good also on toast rounds as a canapé.

BEEF STROGANOV with RICE

3 large onions, sliced
2 tbsps. butter
2 lbs. lean beef cubed
1 can consommé
Salt and pepper
3 cloves garlic, minced
2 tbsps. oil
2 tbsps. flour
2 can tomato paste
1 (8 oz.) can mushrooms
2 cups buttermilk
White rice ring

Serves 6. Fry the onion and garlic in butter and oil. Fry the meat quickly with these. Add the flour, tomato paste, consommé, mushrooms, salt, and pepper. Simmer on top of the stove until meat is done. Add buttermilk. Heat carefully so as not to curdle. Serve in a ring of hot, dry rice.

Paskha is a Russian dessert made of cream cheese, chopped fruits, and nuts.

■

By far the most famous dish with the old Service set in Washington is Gil Allen's Lamb Curry with Rice. Always on Thursday at the Army and Navy Club, this curry is featured. The recipe was originally presented to the Club years ago by Gil Allen, an Army officer returned from the Philippines during the "days of the Empire."

The recipe was given me by the President of the Army and Navy Club, Washigton, D.C. (Reprinted by permission of *Vogue,* Condé Nast Publications, from my own article about Washington.)

GIL ALLEN'S LAMB CURRY and RICE

1 tbsp. butter
1 tbsp. cornstarch
1 tbsp. curry powder
Salt and pepper
1 tsp. onion juice
2 cups milk
1/2 tsp. Worcestershire sauce
2 cups cubed, cooked lamb
Cooked white rice
Grated coconut
Slivered, toasted almonds
Chutney

Serves 2. Make the sauce into a creamy mixture using the first 7 ingredients. Add 2 cups cooked roast of lamb, cubed. Serve hot over flaky, dry rice. Converted rice is used at the Club nowadays. The service is arranged in compartment dishes, the large sections containing the hot rice, generously covered with curried lamb; the two smaller sections have grated, toasted coconut and slivered, toasted almonds. Chutney is the only other side dish. This individual serving arrangement guarantees a hot curry, not so much in taste as in temperature. A tepid curry and rice is inexcusable.

The amount of curry powder depends entirely on the preference of the cook. Some are curry addicts and must have theirs fiery, others prefer it very mild, while the majority take the middle course. The curry at the Club is on the delicate side, but very subtle.

■

Chutneys were Anglo-Indian inspired. This piquant condiment emphasizes the contrast of flavors.

UNCOOKED CHUTNEY

1 lb. dried apricots
1½ lbs. onions
5 hot chilies
Powdered ginger
1 qt. vinegar
1 lb. stoned dates
1½ lbs. white sugar
Nutmeg, cinnamon

Makes about 6 pints. Soak apricots in vinegar for a few minutes. Grind apricots, onions, chilies, and dates together. Add sugar and vinegar with a pinch of salt. A little melted butter, some cinnamon, ginger, and nutmeg may be added. This will keep for months and is easy to make. A friend attached to the South African Embassy in Washington gave it to me.

MIMI'S CHUTNEY

1 pint mild vinegar
2 lbs. brown sugar
8 green apples
2 cloves garlic
1 lb. seedless raisins
2 tbsps. preserved ginger
1/2 tsp. each allspice, cinnamon, nutmeg
Cayenne to taste
Sliced, blanched almonds
1/2 pint water
Salt
8 green pears
1 tsp. mustard seeds
1 lb. currants
6 dry, hot chilies
Paraffin

Makes 8 glasses. Make a syrup of vinegar, water, and brown sugar. Sprinkle peeled, thinly sliced green apples and pears with salt. Add them to syrup. Cook until almost soft, with minced garlic, mustard seed, raisins and currants, chopped ginger, minced chilies, sliced almonds, seasonings, with additional salt to taste. Put in sterilized jelly glasses, top with paraffin. Keeps indefinitely if you have a secret hiding place!

For a homemade chutney, none can surpass this recipe of my mother's. The fruit is green and tastes quite a bit like mangoes.

GRECIAN DOLMAS

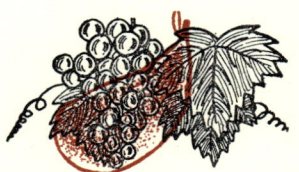

Tender grape leaves
1/2 cup cooked rice
Salt, pepper
1 lb. lamb, ground
Thyme, nutmeg, cinnamon
Spicy tomato paste

Serves 6. Wash grape or cabbage leaves. Place in boiling water for 5 minutes, without cooking. Remove and cool. Have butcher grind meat (minus gristle and fat) 3 times, so that it is like a paste. Combine it with the cooked rice and seasonings, except tomato paste. Mix well with fork. Put a tablespoon of meat mixture in each grape leaf and roll firmly. Roll from stem end, lap sides, and continue to roll tightly. Place in bottom of casserole lined with grape leaves. Arrange dolmas layer over layer. Add ½ cup water, with some tomato paste. Cover with tight lid and simmer 2 hours. Serve with yogurt and lemon wedges. Serving a "salata" of shredded raw white cabbage, shredded pickled beets, and capers, and a tart dressing of vinegar, oil, salt, and mustard, decorated with small, shriveled pickled black olives, is an old Grecian custom.

Iran (formerly Persia) and Iraq, as well as **Armenia**, all have wonderful rice dishes, too numerous for me to list, so I will return to the land of my father's ancestors—Virginia—where the Pages thrived on Brunswick stew.

∎

BRUNSWICK STEW

Serves 6. Steam a large, fat hen in an iron pot out of doors over a hickory-wood fire. Add cut-up onion, carrot, celery, green pepper. Season with salt, pepper, sugar to taste. Add 1 cup butter (lima) beans (if frozen, do not put in until later) at same time as chicken. Let simmer until chicken is half done. Then add 3 white potatoes, cut into cubes, and 1 cup sliced okra. Continue simmering until chicken is tender. Remove chicken, cut into bite-sized pieces, and keep hot. Add 6 ears green corn scraped from cob and several cut-up tomatoes. Cook until thick, add chicken, reheat. Chopped parsley and cayenne are added at last. Serve in deep soup dishes, generously lined with steamed white rice. Or serve rice in a tureen duplicating the one from which stew is ladled.

∎

CANETON MONT-MORENCY

Clean and dress wild duck (one to a person if small variety). Stuff with slices of onion, apple, orange, a stalk of celery, and a clove of garlic. Rub breast with soy sauce and salad oil. Place in baking pan. Roast uncovered in a very hot oven (450°–500°), basting often with California Burgundy wine, using about ½ cup wine per duck. Roasting time is: rare, 15–20 minutes; well-done, 45 minutes. Remove stuffing before serving. Arrange the ducks on a heated platter and serve with plenty of hot wild or white rice.

Now for the Montmorency touch:

Sauce Montmorency

1 No. 2 can black Bing cherries or 1 lb. fresh cherries
3 tbsps. wine vinegar
2 lumps sugar
Brandy or liqueur

Heat the canned cherries, or stew fresh ones with sugar to taste until tender. Separate juice from fruit. In a small pan, reduce the vinegar with the 2 lumps of sugar until it caramelizes. Add cherry juice. Remove the fat from the pan used for roasting the ducks, and dissolve the brown drippings with 4 ounces Coronet brandy or cherry liqueur. Add this to the sauce and simmer a few minutes. Garnish duck with whole, pitted cherries. Serve the sauce separately to pour over the ambrosial slices of duck reposing blissfully on the all-important rice. This amount of sauce is enough for 4.

Pheasant can be prepared this same way. One of the reasons we delight in being residents of Washington, D.C., is the wild-game luncheons served at the Washington Zoo's restaurant to our gourmet group, the "Anteaters." Wild duck and pheasant are favorites with us, and you will surely like this epicurean recipe, especially as it serves a dual purpose. It may readily be adapted to glamorize the domestic, and more accessible, variety. Most sportsmen prefer their game birds rare, but we like to exclaim "Well done!" at *our* work of art!

PERI-PERI CHICKEN from PORTUGUESE EAST AFRICA

Broiling chickens
1/2 cup butter or olive oil
4 crushed chilies
3 cloves of garlic, chopped
1 tsp. chopped parsley
1 tbsp. lemon juice
Cooked white rice

Halve chickens or buy pieces. Make a sauce by melting the butter (or heating oil) in a saucepan with all the ingredients except chickens. Grill the chickens, allowing half to a person, over charcoal. Brush on the sauce (enough for 4 halves) while broiling. Serve chicken and sauce with rice and a tossed green salad of chicory, young spinach leaves, and watercress, with Roquefort dressing. Toasted sesame rolls are fine additions.

■

CURRIED SCALLOPS

2 dozen scallops
1 stick butter (1/2 cup)
1 pint milk
1 tbsp. curry powder
1 tbsp. cornstarch
Salt, nutmeg

Serves 4. Wash and clean scallops well. Put aside. Put milk in saucepan, add butter, salt, curry powder, and cornstarch, mixed together with a little milk. Bring to a slow boil, stirring continually, until a smooth sauce is made. Drop in scallops and heat through quickly. Add nutmeg, and serve in hot rice ring. This is an old Army favorite in Washington. Frozen scallops may be used.

SASATIES

4 lb. leg mutton, cut in cubes
4 lbs. filet of pork, cubed
4 large onions, sliced
1 tbsp. curry powder
1 tsp. salt
1 tbsp. sugar
2 bay leaves, crumbled
1 tbsp. turmeric
Vinegar
Pepper, paprika
Cooked white rice

Serves 16. Place meat and onions in a crockery bowl, seasoning with the salt, pepper, and paprika. Add the rest of the ingredients, using only enough vinegar to cover. Taste; if it seems too acid, add a little water. The mixture should be on the sweet side. Allow to stand for 24 hours. Remove meat and put on skewers, the mutton and pork alternately. Grill over charcoal if possible. Boil the marinade until the onions are tender, and thicken with cornstarch. Serve sauce with the sasaties and bowls of dry, white rice.

Good friends of ours at the South African Embassy here in the nation's capital frequently prepare this delicious dish, native to their country. What a delightful meal-in-itself for Sunday suppers!

For dessert, light and airy, there is Pineapple Ambrosia, also from the South African Embassy. Combine diced orange sections, cubes of canned or fresh pineapple, and grated coconut. Mix with the fruits a little muscatel or white port wine. Chill. At serving time, heap fruit in dessert dishes and top with coconut. Decorate with fresh mint leaves.

SEAFOOD DEEPFREEZE with SPECIAL RICE, BERLIN

Serves 8. Thaw 2 pkgs. frozen fillets of sole and poach them in water just to cover, adding 2 tbsps. tarragon vinegar, 1 tsp. salt, 2 tsps. dehydrated onion chips, several whole black peppercorns, and 2 bay leaves. When almost done, turn off heat and let stand in liquid. In the meantime, boil 2 pkgs. frozen lobster tails in enough salted water to cover. Boil gently for 10 min., drain and remove meat. Cut crosswise in ½ inch slices. Cook two pkgs. frozen broccoli according to directions. Drain and slice lengthwise. Add 2 chopped, hard-cooked eggs to 2 cans undiluted cream of mushroom soup, with sherry, to taste, but do not thin noticeably. Rub soft butter inside Pyrex loaf dish. Line bottom with carefully drained sole cut in serving pieces. Take the onions from the cooking water and add them to the sole. Next scatter pieces of lobster and broccoli for a second layer; sprinkle with lemon juice and paprika. Cover with blended egg and mushroom soup sauce. Continue layers until all is used. Sprinkle grated Parmesan cheese and whole-egg "bought" mayonnaise smoothly and rather thickly over top. Put in pan of water and bake at 350° until bubbly.

Have ready 4 cups cooked, hot white rice (use converted type) to which add 1 whole minced, canned pimiento, 2 tbsps. each of chopped cooked leeks and snipped parsley or chives. Mix lightly. Serve the hot seafood in center of a large, heated, round platter. Surround with the special rice, colorful and pretty. Top all with slivered, blanched almonds and peeled, seedless grapes. Serve with "Brown and Serve" Salt Sticks.

All of these ingredients were purchased at the U.S. Army Commissary and kept available in the freezer for impromptu but important luncheons. If your Very Important People Indeed were not your friends before lunching on this superb dish, they surely must have been afterward!

Kuller-Pfirsich is an effective companion for this luncheon. Prick unpeeled, fresh peaches all over with silver fork. Place one apiece in chilled champagne cobbler goblets. Pour iced dry champagne over peaches and serve. The bubbles on the peach will slowly revolve the peach and impart its flavor to the champagne. This is worthy of a general's lady. I first gave this "Berlin Luncheon," as described, in honor of Mrs. Anthony C. McAuliffe, attractive wife of General "Tony" McAuliffe of Bastogne fame, both life-long friends of ours.

■

From the international atmosphere of our nation's capital comes this warm American human-interest story about our dear friends "Marje and Mike."

As a young Army officer taking the law course at Columbia University, "Mike" Brannon was offered quarters at Bedloe's Island, site of the Statue of Liberty. This island home turned out to be a converted warehouse! But the Brannons and their children were delighted, for Mondays through Fridays the "School Boat" stopped by. Not only the children, but their father, were always on time for the voyage.

Meanwhile, Mrs. Brannon would take a later "Shopping Boat," and at the vast Washington Market in Lower Manhattan, she selected fresh meats, seafood, garden vegetables, and herbs. Returning well before the "School Boat," this busy Army matron would evolve nourishing supper dishes while waiting her seafarers' return.

A favorite dish welcomed by her famished travelers was

called "School Boat Stew" by the youngsters, who particularly enjoyed the tongue-twisting title. Instead of the usual potatoes, they insisted that their special stew have a base of fluffy white rice. The whole family thrived on the following versatile recipe *and* Captain Brannon later became Judge Advocate General of the Army!

■

SCHOOL BOAT STEW

2 lbs. meat (beef, lamb, veal, or poultry)
Bouquet of sweet herbs
Salt, pepper, paprika
Chives
Assorted vegetables
Onion juice, lemon juice
3 cups boiled rice
Cheese
Oil, butter
Gravy

Serves 4. Have butcher select lean meat and cut it into 1½ inch cubes, removing gristle. Brown this in vegetable oil, drain, then add seasonings to taste. Add hot water just to cover. Put lid on heavy skillet or Dutch oven and simmer about 1½ to 2 hours. For flavoring, add 1 sliced, unpeeled carrot, 1 turnip, 1 parsnip, 1 peeled, whole onion (spiked with whole cloves), and 1 peeled, split clove of garlic, together with a small cheesecloth bag containing fresh sweet basil, rosemary, parsley, and majoram. These are all removed when meat is tender. Add water, as it evaporates while cooking. Thicken with about ¼ cup of flour, blended with a little cold water. Add onion and lemon juice to taste. In the meanwhile, cook carrot balls (made with a small vegetable scoop), celery cubes, green-pepper slices, green peas or stringbeans, lima beans, and whole, peeled, baby onions. Steam rather than boil them, in as little salt water as possible. Here you can use your imagination and add vegetables in season. Combine the meat and drained vegetables. Use vegetable water to augment gravy. Line a slightly buttered casserole with the dry, fluffy, cooked rice, about 1 inch deep all around. Fill center with the stew. Do not make really moist. Reserve extra gravy to pass at table. Cover the casserole with rice. Dot top with paprika, snipped parsley or chives, pimiento, and cheese. Cover with aluminum foil and bake until heated thoroughly. Uncover and brown until golden and bubbly.

After this meal, the Brannon children prepared their own "Liberty Sundaes" with appropriate colors—cherries or strawberries first, scoops of vanilla ice cream, and a topping of blueberries. The parents preferred red apples and cheese with coffee.

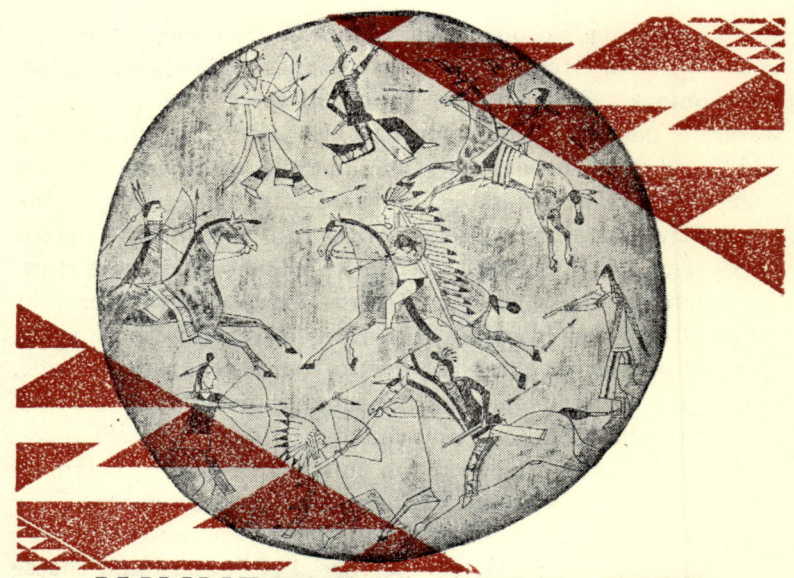

MINNESOTA WILD RICE

■ ■ ■ Almost all the wild rice in the world is grown in Minnesota. Some is grown in western Wisconsin, and some in Canada, but that which is marketed is in large part Minnesota rice. The state law in Minnesota requires that no white man can harvest the wild rice—only the Indian can do so. The rice (ma-no-men) was the staple food of the Sioux and Chippewa Indians, and possession of camp sites from which it could be harvested was the cause of major battles between these two tribes. Today, the large processing companies buy the wild rice from the Indians as they bring it in to shore in their canoes. Wild rice is not actually rice but the seed of shallow-water grass. It has a delicious flavor and goes especially well with wild game, as a dressing or an accompaniment. It is well worth the extra expense, for these wild, spindly, grey grains expand to twice their size when cooked.

It is impossible to give a hard and fast rule for the cooking of wild rice. As the name implies, the grain is found in a wild state and is not cultivated. The kernels vary as to length, thickness, and hardness. When cooked, wild rice has absorbed the maximum amount of water, has fluffed up, and is ready to eat.

The quick method of cooking wild rice is to wash the rice several times with cold water, add 4 cups salted water per cup of rice and allow to simmer for 20 minutes, covered. Do not overcook rice. It is at its best when cooked slowly so it will retain its nutty flavor.

WILD RICE with CRAB MEAT

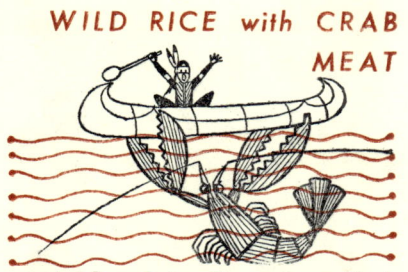

6 thin onion slices
6 thin green-pepper slices
1 bay leaf, pepper
Bread crumbs
1 clove garlic
3 sprigs parsley
6 eggs
1 5-oz. can crab meat
3 cups cooked wild rice

Serves 6. Put the above vegetables into 2 cups salted water and simmer 30 minutes. Strain out vegetables and save liquid. Add 1 (5 oz.) can best crab meat to the liquid, simmer 10 minutes. Add 3 cups cooked wild rice, mix well. Taste for seasoning. Divide into 6 ramekins. Press a round soup spoon in center of each ramekin to make a well, drop a raw, fresh egg into each cavity. Cover each with buttered bread crumbs. Brown under broiler. When eggs are well poached, serve immediately. **An excellent luncheon dish.**

FRIED WILD RICE with ALMONDS

1/2 cup salad oil
1 clove garlic, minced
Salt, pepper, paprika
1/2 cup chopped green pepper
1/2 cup chopped onion
1 cup sliced almonds
3 cups cooked wild rice

Serves 6. Sauté vegetables in oil, add cooked rice, seasonings, and almonds. Mix well and fry carefully, stirring constantly. Serve with veal stew.

■

BAKED WILD RICE with OYSTERS and SHRIMP

1 can frozen oysters
1 pkg. frozen shrimp
1 No. 2 can tomatoes
Salt, pepper, paprika
1 bay leaf, crumbled
2 tsps. lemon juice
1 onion, chopped
1 tbsp. chopped fresh basil
1 can sliced mushrooms, or fresh mushrooms
4 tbsps. butter
1 cup raw wild rice

Serves 6. Defrost the frozen oysters and shrimp, reserving liquid. Remove shells from shrimp and de-vein them. Fry drained oysters in half the butter until edges curl. Sauté sliced mushrooms, if you are using fresh ones, with onion in remaining butter. Combine raw rice, oysters, shrimp, mushrooms, onion, lemon juice, and seasonings with liquid from seafood and tomatoes. The liquids should give sufficient moisture to cook the well-washed wild rice. If more is

needed, add vegetable juice. Place in buttered casserole and bake at 350° until rice is cooked. The whole dish should be on the dry side when served. A watercress and sliced, sweet Bermuda onion salad, with cottage-cheese balls and paprika-French dressing, goes perfectly with this dish. Bread sticks and coffee complete the ensemble.

2 cups wild rice
1 cup milk
1 stick butter (1/2 cup)
2 tbsps. flour
2 tbsps. sherry
1 lb. fresh mushrooms
2 cans condensed cream of mushroom soup
Worcestershire sauce
Lemon juice
Salt, pepper, paprika

WILD RICE and MUSHROOM RING

Serves 10. Cook the rice according to directions on package and pack it into a well-buttered ring mold, keeping the ring covered over hot water. Make a sauce of the cream of mushroom soup, diluted with the milk. Slice the washed mushrooms crosswise including stems, add seasonings, and sauté in butter, sprinkling the flour over them. Cook until almost tender. Add mushrooms to sauce. Taste for salt, as the canned soups are rather salty in themselves. When ready to serve, unmold the wild-rice ring onto a round, hot platter and fill center with creamed mushrooms. Cubed, cooked chicken, veal, or lamb may be added to the mushroom mixture if desired. Garnish with watercress. This makes a wonderful buffet supper dish, accompanied by a salad of fresh fruits, assorted cheeses, and crackers.

HERBED WILD RICE

1 cup wild rice
1/2 tsp. poultry seasoning
Pinch of thyme
1/4 cup chopped onion
1/4 cup chopped chives
1/4 cup butter
4 cups chicken broth
1/4 cup chopped celery
1 tsp. salt

Wash rice thoroughly. Melt butter, sauté onions and celery until golden. Add rice, salt, and herbs. Simmer slowly, covered, in the chicken broth until tender. Fine for stuffing fowl or duck, wild game birds, and with cold meats.

WILD RICE and SWEETBREADS

Serves 6. Soak 2 pairs calves' sweetbreads, in cold water for 30 minutes. Drain. Place in boiling water to which add 2 tbsps. vinegar, 4 peppercorns, 1 bay leaf, and 1 tsp. salt. Cover and simmer until tender, about 25 minutes. Drain and blanch the sweetbreads by plunging them into ice water (with ice cubes) for 10 minutes. Clean by skinning and discarding tubes. Sweetbreads should not be pink. Cut into medium pieces. Place in saucepan with 1 can cream of mushroom soup, add ½ lb. fresh mushrooms, sliced and sautéed in butter, some nutmeg, and 2 tbsps. sherry. Add 1 cup diced baked ham. Have prepared a hot wild-rice ring on a hot, round platter and fill with the sweetbread-mushroom-ham combination.

Another filling is chicken livers, sautéed in butter, with some onion juice and chopped parsley. Taste for seasonings.

Many epicures add brandy to taste. Combine the chicken livers with the cream of mushroom soup and blend well. Put in center of the wild-rice ring. The creamed chicken livers may also be combined with cooked wild rice, seasoned with herbs, salt, and pepper, and cooked together in a casserole. Top with butter and bake 15 minutes until heated through. Serve from casserole, with endive and chopped hard-cooked egg salad.

GREEN CASSEROLE with WILD RICE

1 cup chopped frozen or fresh spinach
1 pkg. frozen chopped broccoli
1 minced onion
4 beaten eggs
Salt, pepper, paprika
Nutmeg, allspice
1 cup cooked wild rice
1 clove garlic, minced
Parmesan cheese
4 tbsps. olive oil
1 cup cut-up boiled ham

Serves 6. Sauté drained, chopped, thawed frozen spinach and broccoli with onion and garlic in olive oil. Season with salt, pepper, paprika, nutmeg, and allspice to taste. Add the cooked wild rice and cut-up boiled ham; brown lightly without mashing the rice. Put into a buttered casserole, adding the beaten eggs. Bake at 350° until eggs begin to set. Top with grated, fresh Parmesan cheese. Put under boiler until cheese is bubbly and light brown. Serve at once. Cooked tiny sausages may be included. A very delicate luncheon dish, with deviled egg and tuna salad and red wine.

INDIAN FRY BREAD

2 cups flour
3 tsps. baking powder
1 tsp. salt
1 cup milk, plus 2 tbsps., approx.
Deep, hot fat

Makes 8–10 pieces. Mix and sift the flour with the baking powder and salt. Lightly stir in about 1 cup milk, adding about 2 tbsps. more to make a thick batter. Drop by tablespoons into deep, hot fat, and fry (in wire basket) until golden brown on both sides. Drain on absorbent paper. A splendid accompaniment to wild-rice dishes is this Indian Fry Bread, invented by an Indian girl named Wanonia. (I am able to give you this recipe through the courtesy of *Seventeen,* published by Triangle Publications Corporation. My gratitude is due also to the Mille Lacs Maple Products Company for their suggestions for using wild rice.)

▪▪▪ TO THE WEST

MEXICAN HOLIDAY

■ ■ ■ My husband and I spent two gay months in the suburbs of Mexico City, visiting three young bachelor Army officers. They had leased a modernistic villa next to the home of Diego Rivera, the Mexican muralist.

The Indian-Mexican cook, a flighty person, was forever running to the *mercado* just before breakfast for 5 eggs, one-fourth kilo each of coffee, sugar, and butter, and five rolls. Then in the middle of breakfast, she would dash to the open-air market for another fourth-kilo of coffee, just in case the Americanos wanted a second cup. What mad housekeeping that was! But, on the whole, what a lark for us.

One particular evening I shall never forget. The bachelors had invited a lovely Mexican señorita, whose father was a high government official, to dine with us. All three were smitten with her, but so far she had refused their dinner invitations. Now that a married woman was on hand, she had agreed to accept their hospitality.

At the dinner table, after we had finished our soup, Ofelia carried in a large platter triumphantly and placed it in front of me. "Huachinango!" she announced proudly. We exclaimed with delight at the large, baked red snapper, decorated artistically with lime halves, tomatoes, and watercress. It was so beautifully glazed, so delicately browned. But, to our dismay, the masterpiece had never been scaled! The only way we could rid ourselves of the pesky scales in our mouths was to wash them down with still more vino! To us, the one saving grace was the delicious stuffing of Mexican Rice. Sad to say, the señorita never dined there again!

■

HUACHINANGO VERACRUZANO or RED SNAPPER, VERACRUZ

Clean, wash, and *scale* a large, freshly caught, red snapper. Stuff the inside with savory Mexican Rice (see below), and spread the outside thickly with bacon fat. Pat in some sifted flour to make a thin coat. Then put fish into uncovered baking pan on several strips of bacon or salt pork, but use no water. Make a sauce of peeled, sliced tomatoes, cut-up onions and garlic, and thinly sliced, peeled chili peppers (or use prepared "pepperoni"). Put this over and around fish. Cook for 30 minutes, then sprinkle chopped green olives over all. Salt and pepper is shaken over top. Remember that bacon fat is salty. Put back and bake in oven 15 more minutes. Temperature is 350°. Serve with wedges of lime, strips of pimiento, capers, parsley, watercress. Allow ½ lb. per person.

■

3 cups raw white rice
2 cups canned tomatoes
1 onion, chopped finely
1 clove garlic
1 green pepper
A few celery stalks
2 tsps. chili powder
2 cups canned consommé diluted with 2 cups water
Salt, pepper, orégano, paprika

MEXICAN-RICE STUFFING for FISH, FOWL, or WILD GAME BIRDS

Sauté rice in olive oil in heavy skillet. Keep stirring until rice is quite brown. Add tomatoes, garlic, pepper, and celery. Sprinkle chili powder on rice. Add consommé. Season. Boil fast at first, then reduce heat and simmer for 20 minutes. Stuff fish with the aromatic rice. This is enough for a large fish.

■

In Mexico *mole* is their classic sauce. It is made by sautéeing chopped onions and garlic in olive oil and adding chili powder. A little powdered chocolate is also used to lend an Aztec flavor. Serve on rice, with turkey hash, or leftover chicken, beef, or lamb. Cut-up avocados and lime juice are exotic additions.

BAKED FISH with ALMOND SAUCE

Serves 6. Arrange several sliced onions, 1 crumbled bay leaf, some thyme, orégano, a few whole cloves, and black peppercorns in bottom of oiled baking dish. Take 4 lbs. whole white fish and cover with fresh lime juice, salt, pepper, and olive oil. Let stand in baking dish, turning fish. Grind 1 cup blanched almonds, add enough milk to make a thick paste. Add to it 1 cup grated Parmesan cheese and ½ cup sherry. Pour all this inside and outside of fish. Sprinkle with bread crumbs, olive oil, paprika, and chopped parsley. Bake at 350°, 45 minutes. At serving time, sprinkle with freshly grated nutmeg. Decorate with avocado and tomato crescents. Serve hot Mexican Rice as the other half of the meal.

ALBONDIGAS con ARROZ or MEAT BALLS with RICE

1 lb. ground meat
2 onions, chopped
1 egg, beaten
1 tsp. chili powder
1/2 tsp. orégano
1 clove garlic, minced
3 tbsps. flour
Salt, pepper, thyme, paprika
Tomato juice and paste

Serves 4-6. Mix 1 lb. ground beef, veal, lamb, or pork with onions (sautéed), egg, chili powder, orégano, garlic, flour, salt, pepper, thyme, and paprika. Roll into small balls, sear quickly in hot fat, cover with tomato juice, and cook slowly 1 hour. Make a sauce by adding tomato paste. Serve hot over dry, flaky white rice.

A watermelon, the flesh scooped out and made into little balls, with chunks of fresh pineapple and other tropical fruits, heightened with wine or cognac, is very refreshing when served icy cold and goes well with this recipe. Decorate with fresh mint leaves.

A simple Mexican meal is Chili con Carne with beans served over white rice. Another is Sopa Seca (Mexican Rice to which plump raisins and almonds have been added), served with chick peas (garbanzos), soaked and cooked with chopped pork, onions, garlic, and tomatoes. These are both very satisfying and inexpensive fare. One lives well in Mexico. Viva Mexico!

CANAL ZONE CASSEROLES

■■■ When winter is in full play in Washington, D.C., I like to recall the sundown hour in the Panama Canal Zone. In the high-ceilinged Army quarters where we visited, the rooms were filled with ginger blossoms. On the wide screened verandas, many hanging baskets of feathery fern and potted palms created a perfect setting for the starched, white uniforms and filmy summer frocks.

Against a tropical background of coconut trees, oleander bushes, and poinsettias, deft white-coated servants passed hors d'oeuvres, cigarettes, and cooling drinks. After the cocktail party, our hostess had thoughtfully arranged to have a Panamanian *cazuela* (casserole) ready for us. This gave every one energy to dance the night through with verve.

ESTOFADO con TOMATE y ARROZ or STEWED CHICKEN with TOMATOES and RICE

1 chicken, cut up, and browned
2 tbsps. olive oil
6 tomatoes, sliced
Paprika, cayenne
Pinch of saffron
Salt, rosemary, orégano, pepper
1 tbsp. raisins
Chopped green olives
2 onions, diced
1 green pepper, chopped
2 white potatoes, diced
1 slice toast, diced
1 cup dry white wine
2 cloves garlic, mashed
Browned, cooked rice

Serves 8. Heat olive oil in heavy skillet; add onions, green pepper; cook lightly; add tomatoes. Season highly. Cover and simmer for 10 minutes. Add the browned chicken; cook until almost tender; then put in the cubed, raw potatoes, the toast, raisins (plumped), white wine, chopped green olives, and garlic mashed in mortar or garlic press. Taste for seasoning. If more liquid is needed, add tomato or vegetable juice. There should not be too much liquid, however. Cover and simmer until chicken and vegetables are cooked through. If your skillet is not large enough, transfer to an earthenware casserole when chicken is added.

This dish is always served with browned rice: brown 2 cups raw white rice in bacon fat or olive oil in heavy skillet. Toss browned rice into a pot containing 4 cups furiously boiling, salted water. Reduce heat immediately and boil rice gently. When it is tender but not soft, place rice in a colander over hot water. Cover rice with a clean cloth. Steam until dry. This is a perfect twosome for an "after-the-cocktail-party" constitutional.

EGGS and RICE before REVEILLE

1 small jar chipped beef
Grated cheese
Cayenne, saffron, cinnamon, nutmeg
Butter
1 cup tomatoes, drained
Onion juice
8 beaten eggs
Dry white rice

Serves 6. Shred dried beef; add tomatoes, cheese, onion juice. Melt sufficient butter and in it toss the beef with all ingredients but eggs. Beat the eggs until fluffy; add to beef-tomato mixture. Season, but omit salt, since dried beef is salty. Cook until eggs are set and creamy, stirring as for scrambled eggs. Serve on dry white rice. This should be concocted with a deft hand so as not to curdle. Another after-dancing "pick-me-up."

ARROZ con SEÑORITAS a la LINDA or RICE and LITTLE SCALLOPS

2 cups raw rice
4 cups water
Salt and pepper
3 dozen "señoritas" (little scallops)
1 tsp. chili powder
1 clove garlic
2 tbsps. shortening

Serves 6. Place shortening in earthenware casserole; fry the garlic, removing when brown; add the "señoritas" (frozen Long Island Bay scallops can be substituted for the "señoritas"); add chili powder; sauté a few moments; add water, salt, and pepper to taste; bring to a boil; add rice. Cook over low heat, taking care that rice remains whole, adding a few drops of fresh lemon juice to keep it well grained.

Spanish slaw is an inspired addition to this "menuette." Shred young, green cabbage, soak it in ice water, drain, and pat dry between paper towels. Add to it thinly sliced green pepper, shaved carrots, celery, onion, and some celery seed. Mix with an olive-oil and wine-vinegar dressing. Decorate with canned pimiento "stars" and lime-soaked avocado strips.

ARROZ con PATO or RICE with DUCK

2 tender young ducks, cut up
2 garlic cloves, mashed
1 cup bacon fat
Salt, pepper, orégano
1 wineglass sherry
Boiling water
1 pkg. frozen green peas
2 tsps. chili powder
2 cups raw brown rice

Serves 4–6. Melt fat in deep casserole; add mashed garlic; brown; add chili powder, salt, pepper, and orégano. Fry the pieces of duck in this mixture. When browned on both sides, add 4 cups water, bring to a boil, cover, lower flame, and simmer until duck is almost done. Then add rice, continuing to cook slowly, covered. There should be 4 cups duck broth in which to cook the rice. Cook frozen green peas, add to rice when latter is dry. Flavor with sherry (or brandy). Serve very hot. Sliced firm tomatoes, sprinkled with chopped green onions and served icy cold, make a pretty side dish. Hard rolls and vino tinto (red wine) add gaiety.

SOPA SECA de ARROZ con HUEVOS or FRIED RICE with EGGS

2 tbsps. olive oil
1 cup raw rice
1 onion, chopped
1/2 tsp. salt
Shake of cayenne
1/2 tsp. powdered saffron
6 eggs
Chopped parsley
Canned consommé

Serves 6. Sauté raw rice and onion together in olive oil, adding more oil if necessary. Stir until brown, add salt and 2 cups boiling diluted consommé. Stir, season, cover, and simmer until rice is done but not soft. Remove cover and make depressions for eggs in rice. Break an egg into each well. Return cover and cook until eggs are well set. Sprinkle with chopped parsley. A fine "midnight snack."

■

PESCADO con ARROZ or FISH with RICE

3 tbsps. vinegar
6 each whole cloves and peppercorns
1 can consommé
1 bay leaf, cayenne
3 cups fresh, firm fish, flaked
1 tbsp. flour
1 onion, sliced
1 clove garlic, minced
1 cup canned tomatoes, strained
Hot, cooked white rice

Serves 6. Simmer spices, onion, and garlic in vinegar 15 minutes. Let steep, covered. Strain, add undiluted consommé, thickened with flour. Add strained, heated tomatoes, bring to the boiling point, then stir in the flaked fish and heat through, being careful not to break. Cooked seafood may be spiced this same way. Taste for salt and pepper. Serve hot on buttered rice cooked in consommé, made attractive to the eye (and appetite) with chopped pimiento and parsley or chives.

Fish is the national emblem of the Republic of Panama, and many dishes have fish and rice in combination. Add cut-up tomatoes, onions, garlic, herbs, a bit of saffron, and olive oil to any baked fish. Always serve with rice sautéed in olive oil and then steamed, or rice cooked in consommé.

WEST-INDIAN SPANISH RICE

■■■ In three Caribbean countries, Cuba, the Dominican Republic, and Puerto Rico, everything reflects the Spanish influence—the language, the customs, and the food. You will find Spanish specialities such as *paella* or *arroz con pollo* served with West Indian fruits and vegetables (papaya, guava, mango, plantain, yuca, and rice). Coconut milk, local rum, the juices of limes and sour oranges lend a special, subtle flavor to drinks and food. Spanish hospitality is lavish and lingering. A typical fiesta begins at nine and lasts until dawn, with a mammoth banquet to sustain guests who have been dancing the fast, rhythmic *merengue*. Highspot of the feast may be a whole roast suckling pig or the famous stew, *sancocho*, served with steaming white rice.

Sancocho is one of the many Latin American versions of Spain's traditional stew, the *olla podrida,* which is to Spain what the *pot-au-feu* is to France. Olla podrida, which means, literally, an olla (cooking pot) filled with a podrida (assortment) of meat, fowl or fish, fresh vegetables, rice, herbs, and spices, is a marvelous main dish for a buffet or supper party. There are no conventional rules to the recipe: you can experiment with different combinations of meat, seafood, vegetables, and rice, and make your podrida as savory and hearty as the budget allows. Substitute a modern earthenware casserole for the olla, and, if you are in a hurry, use a pressure cooker to cut cooking time for fowl or less choice cuts of meat.

Start this Spanish meal with an apéritif of pale, dry sherry and serve the stew in deep pottery plates with crusty, unbuttered bread; chilled salad greens, shining with olive oil; and a carafe of wine. A chilled white wine goes well with hot one-dish native meals, or if you prefer a more robust wine, choose a claret. Finish with fresh fruit, black coffee, and brandy.

If you have seen the Caribbean islands first-hand, you will recall the intensity of blue sea and sky, the brilliance of foliage and flowers, pink and white powdery beaches. You can capture some of the refreshing tropical background on your own terrace. Copy such cool ideas as airy wrought-iron chairs, a marble-topped table, a screen of feathery plants. Take the windswept blues and greens of the Caribbean for your table setting and add a seashell centerpiece. Serve rum and lime cocktails, "frutas de la mar" (seafood —or, more picturesquely, fruits of the sea) with saffron rice. For background music: a stack of Spanish dance records on the hi-fi.

Following is my collection of authentic and exotic rice

recipes, gathered while living in these Spanish-speaking countries. (Reprinted by permission of *House & Garden*, Condé Nash Publications, from my own *Caribbean Cook Book*.) "¡Buen provecho!" as they say in Spanish.

ARROZ con FRIJOLES or RICE and BEANS

Serves about 6. These are the standard staple of every Latin American meal. As in Haiti, the dried congo or pinto bean is used, but you can substitute the black, or turtle bean, or the red kidney variety. The beans are not soaked overnight, as this process detracts from their flavor and color. Instead, rinse 2 cups beans well and cover with water in an earthenware cazuela, or cooking pot. Add 1 tbsp. olive oil, some minced garlic and onion, a pinch of thyme, salt, cayenne to taste. Simmer slowly for 6 hours or longer, adding more water as needed. To shorten time, you may use a pressure cooker, but do not mash beans. Beans should be tender, but not broken. Serve, with a little bean liquid, over dry, white, cooked rice, passed in a companion earthenware dish at the table. One is never served without the other. The native bean is very small, round, and a dark mahogany color. These are found in Spanish stores. If you are feeling affluent, add cut-up raw ham or bacon for more flavor.

Our servants kept a pot each of beans and rice warming continually on the charcoal stoves in the Dominican Republic, where my parents lived for twenty years. Whenever anyone felt the urge, in went the dippers, made of gourds, to fill the servants' plates and stomachs! This was not limited to the natives in the Caribbean. We all enjoyed this savory combination. It is known, in Spanish-speaking countries, as "moros y cristianos," the dark bean being the Moors of ancient Spain, and the white rice, the Christians, or Spaniards.

CARNE con BERENJENAS Y ARROZ or MEAT LOAF with EGGPLANT and RICE

1½ lbs. ground round of beef
1/2 lb. sausage meat
1 large eggplant, boiled and cubed
4 stewed tomatoes, or 1 large can tomatoes
1 tbsp. Worcestershire sauce
3 hard-cooked eggs
2 onions, chopped
1 clove garlic, minced
1 canned pimiento
2 eggs, beaten
Salt, pepper, orégano
2 cups cooked rice

Serves 8. Season the meats and mix together. Add peeled, boiled, and drained eggplant cubes. Sauté onions and garlic in butter, add to meat. Add tomatoes, chopped pimiento, and beaten eggs. Then mix in the dry, cooked rice with a silver fork so as not to mash. Stir carefully together. Put into 2 greased oven-proof glass meat-loaf dishes, not filling full. Bake at 325° for 1½ hours. Hard-boiled eggs, shelled and left whole, may be inserted end to end in center of loaf, so that egg slice appears in each portion when sliced. An even more attractive effect is to pickle the shelled eggs overnight in beet-juice and vinegar with pickling spices.

SOPA de ARROZ con CREMA or CREAMED RICE SOUP

1 onion, chopped
1/2 cup raw rice
1/2 tsp. saffron
1 tsp. tarragon
2 egg yolks
1 clove garlic, minced
1 cup celery tops, chopped
5 cups chicken broth
Salt, white pepper
Paprika, nutmeg
1 cup light cream, heated

Serves 6. Steam onion, garlic, celery tops in broth 15 minutes. Let stand until broth has absorbed flavors; strain. Add rice, paprika, powdered saffron, and tarragon. Cook gently, covered, until rice is swollen and tender. Add more hot canned chicken broth, if necessary, to make the 5 cups. Just before serving, beat egg yolks into tureen, grinding nutmeg over them. Pour hot cream and boiling broth from a height over yolks. Beat briskly with whisk. Serve in deep soup plates with garlic-flavored croutons, fried in butter. Use garlic powder to flavor them.

■

CHORIZOS con ARROZ or BROWN RICE with SPANISH SAUSAGES

6 Spanish sausages
2 cups brown rice
Salt, paprika
2 tbsps. bacon fat
Pineapple
Avocado
Fresh lime juice

Serves 6. Cover the Spanish garlic-flavored sausages with water and bring to a boil in heavy pot. Cover and simmer until they are tender. Remove sausage and slice crosswise.

Increase remaining liquid to 4 cups by adding water. Bring to a boil, add brown rice, cook slowly, covered, until rice is done and dry. Brown the sliced sausages with sliced fresh or canned pineapple in bacon fat. Drain on brown paper. Surround mound of hot brown rice with sausages and pineapple. Decorate with avocado slices, sprinkled with fresh lime juice, salt, and paprika.

FILETES de PESCADO con ARROZ or POACHED FISH FILLETS with RICE

6 fish fillets
3/4 cup dry white wine
1/4 cup light rum
1/2 cup olive oil
1 tbsp. capers
Salt and pepper
Grated Parmesan cheese
1 clove garlic, minced
1 can cream of mushroom soup, undiluted
Steaming rice

Serves 6. Poach fillets in white wine and rum, adding water to cover. Sauté garlic clove in oil, pour both over seasoned, drained, poached fish. Keep hot in casserole lined with the cooked rice. Reduce wine liquid to ½ cup. Mix smoothly into undiluted cream of mushroom soup (modernized version of Spanish cookery). Pour over fish. Sprinkle grated Parmesan cheese and capers over top and bake at 350° until golden brown.

If a more elaborate dish is desired, add some cooked shrimp and 2 beaten egg yolks, mixed with 2 tbsps. sherry, to the mixture of wine and mushroom soup. This rich dish is balanced by the flaky rice border which surrounds the poached fillets.

CAMARONES PICANTES con ARROZ or SPICY SHRIMP with RICE

Steam desired number of fresh or frozen shrimp. Shell and de-vein. Fry quickly in olive oil. Remove, and put them on an oven-proof platter. Sprinkle shrimp with crumbled chervil, dry or wild majoram (orégano), thyme, cumin seed, and powdered saffron. Next, add grated, tangy cheese and put the platter under broiler. Serve hot with a peppery bottled sauce. A bowl of hot white rice is a must. The rice is served first from a deep bowl, and the spicy shrimp give the crowning touch.

■

ARROZ VERDE or GREEN RICE

1 cup crumbled fried bacon or ham bits
1/2 cup olive oil
2 cups cooked white rice
Salt, white pepper
2 eggs, beaten
1 cup milk
1/2 green pepper, shredded
2 cloves garlic, minced
1 cup each parsley and chives, minced
1 cup grated Parmesan cheese

Serves 6. Mix rice with seasonings. Sauté green pepper and garlic in oil. Pour pepper and oil over rice. Add parsley and chives. Beat milk and eggs together, mix with rice. Put in greased baking dish, top with cheese and bacon or ham bits. Bake at 350° for 30 minutes until egg mixture is set and top is light brown. Chopped watercress, young, green spinach leaves, green onion tops (or bottled, dry, shredded green onions) may be used with the parsley and chives, all minced together to achieve a brilliant green rice dish.

■

AJIS DULCES RELLENOS con ARROZ or GREEN-RICE STUFFED PEPPERS

Parboil desired number of Bell peppers. De-vein and remove seeds, leaving peppers whole. Fill with the above Green Rice. Put peppers in baking dish containing a little hot water. Bake at 350° until well heated through. Cut-up bananas, soaked currants or raisins, and slivered almonds may be included in both the casserole of green rice and the stuffed peppers. Guava jelly and hot cornbread completes a perfect "little meal."

■

RIÑONES en JEREZ con ARROZ or SHERRIED KIDNEYS with RICE

1 pair veal kidneys
1 onion, minced
Creamed watercress
2 tbsps. olive oil
1/2 cup dry sherry
Juice of 1 lemon
Steamed white rice

Serves 4. Sauté onion, add sliced, cleaned kidneys. Season, add sherry. Cook over low heat until kidneys are tender. Serve over steamed rice with creamed watercress (add 1 cup chopped watercress, lightly sautéed in butter, to 1/2 cup undiluted cream of mushroom soup; season with a touch of grated mace). A splendid Sunday or holiday breakfast dish with cornbread made with coconut milk and grated coconut.

ARROZ con PESCADO or FISH with SEASONED RICE

4 lbs. swordfish
6 whole cloves
6 black peppercorns
2 cups cooked rice
1/2 cup olive oil
1½ cups raw, chopped spinach
Juice of 1 lime
Salt, paprika
Pinch each of thyme, tarragon
1/2 cup sautéed chopped onion

Serves 8. Put skinned swordfish, cut into 2-inch pieces, in cheesecloth bag, in gently boiling, salted water. Add cloves and peppercorns. Simmer until fish is almost done, but still firm. Drain, remove cloves and peppercorns, and add fish to cooked rice. Lightly sauté all with olive oil; add raw chopped spinach. Season with lime juice, thyme, tarragon, salt, paprika, and onion. Heat through on top of stove in earthenware casserole. Serve a pineapple sherbet, topped with grated coconut, for a provocative duet.

■

LANGOSTINAS y ARROZ en CONCHAS or PRAWN and RICE in SCALLOP SHELLS

Drop desired number of prawn or crayfish (2 per serving), or jumbo shrimp (4 per serving), in gently boiling, salted water containing 2 peeled cloves of garlic and a dash of cayenne pepper. Cook 12 minutes. Cool, crack, and remove meat from shellfish. Reduce liquid in which they have cooked, adding the shells, whole cloves, caraway seeds, chopped onion, and black peppercorns. For 6 servings: make 2½ cups white sauce, using strained shrimp liquor and 1 can undiluted cream of celery soup. Season with cayenne and salt. Put layer of cut-up prawns into buttered, individual, scallop shells. Add a layer of cooked white rice, flecked with chopped chives and pimiento, and cover tops with the sauce. Any combination of fish or shellfish may be used. A crisp salad of endive with grapefruit and avocado slices and a tart Roquefort-French dressing will be lauded.

■

ARROZ AMARILLO or YELLOW RICE

Serves 6. Add 1 tsp. powdered saffron to 2 cups raw rice with 1 tsp. salt, 4 cups canned chicken broth (or make broth with chicken bouillon cubes). Stir in 2 tbsps. butter, bring to a boil, then cook gently, covered, until dry and fluffy. Turmeric may be added to give a yellow tinge, but it does not approach saffron in flavor. Saffron may be bought in Spanish, Mexican, or Italian grocery stores. Saffron also comes in threads, which must be soaked in melted butter or hot liquid before being added to rice. By adding anything suitable on hand in the refrigerator you may create a baked casserole dish. To the cooked yellow rice, add cooked sausage meat, cooked green peas, pimiento strips, and sliced green olives. Any leftover cooked meats, poultry, fish, or seafood, with added raisins, chopped nuts, fried, minced garlic, onions, capers, and cheese, and you have a snappy, delicious Spanish-type feast in a matter of minutes. Yellow rice does the trick.

PAELLA with RICE

1 large fat hen
1/2 cup olive oil
6 chorizos (Spanish sausages), sliced
1 cup cooked shrimp
12 mussels, or whole little neck clams
1 cup onions, chopped
2 cloves garlic, minced
Orégano, tarragon, fines herbes, salt, white pepper, paprika, saffron
2 cups canned tomatoes
1 package frozen peas
Pimiento
Artichoke hearts
2 cups raw white rice

Serves 8–10. Cover hen with seasoned water, simmer in large, heavy pot with lid on. When tender, cool, cut into good-sized pieces, discarding bones. Separate some white from dark meat and reserve. Sauté onions and garlic in oil, add to 4 cups hot chicken broth. Bring to a boil, add rice with a pinch each of the seasonings given. Taste for salt, add chicken, omitting the reserved white meat. Add sausage slices and tomatoes. Cover and simmer until rice is dry and liquid absorbed. Cook frozen peas separately until just tender and bright green. Add to Paella. Next, add cooked pink shrimp, shelled. Put in the canned or fresh mussels and the fresh clams, which have been steamed until their shells have popped open. Put the extra white meat on top. Decorate with pimiento and tiny-sized artichoke hearts. Serve on a large, heated platter, or in a cazuela. The Spaniards in Old Spain use eels, lobster, crab meat, and fried eggplant strips in addition. This is truly a wonderful party dish.

There was a gourmet Spanish king who doted on creating late supper dishes in his palace apartment for his lights of love. One of the best concoctions he ever dreamed up is the above modified "Paella." His Majesty named this tangy combination of chicken and "fruits of the sea" and rice "Para Ella" (For Her), to please his favorite enamorata of the moment. The Arabs carried rice into Spain under the name of "Aruz," and it became the most beloved of all Spanish dishes.

■

GARBANZOS Y ARROZ or CHICK PEAS and RICE

2 lbs. garbanzos (chick peas)
6 onions, sliced
1 green pepper, chopped
1 green cabbage
2 cups raw white rice
Ham hock with ham
4 cloves garlic, minced
1 tsp. paprika; salt, cayenne to taste
Celery and mustard seed
Chopped parsley and pimiento

Serves 8. Soak garbanzos overnight with a good-sized ham hock having plenty of ham, a sliced onion, and a garlic clove. The next morning simmer in same water on top of stove with more onions, garlic, green pepper, and seasonings. Cook until ham is done and garbanzos almost tender. Add rice (there should be 4 cups liquid) and chopped green cabbage. Cook until liquid is absorbed. Sliced Spanish sausages may also be cooked with this dish. Decorate with parsley and pimiento. Garbanzos and rice must not be mashed.

As we have seen in our travels, beans are combined with rice in many countries. In India, it is the lentil which makes up the duet. In South Carolina, it is the cow pea, or black-eyed pea, and rice. In Texas and in Mexico, *frijoles con arroz* are combined just as they are in Haiti and other Caribbean countries. In the British West Indies, we will see "pigeon pease" and rice. All varieties are economical, satisfying, and nutritious ... and perfectly delicious. With any of them, a citrus fruit salad, with tart dressing, gives the right balance.

■

POLLO CASTELLANO or CHICKEN from CASTILE

1 chicken, 5 lbs.
1 chopped onion
1/2 green pepper, shredded
2 cloves garlic, minced
1/2 cup currants, soaked
Dry white wine
Parsley, tarragon
Blanched almonds
4 cups cooked white rice

Serves 8. Simmer whole chicken in water to cover, with seasoning. Add onion, garlic, green pepper. Remove chicken when tender. Save broth, discard bones, and keep meat in serving slices. Make sauce from chicken broth, reduced to 2 cups. Add ½ cup wine, currants, parsley, and crumbled tarragon. Heat through. If thickening is needed, combine 1 tbsp. cornstarch with 2 tbsps. wine and add to sauce. Put the hot chicken slices in center of steaming rice ring. Pour sauce over chicken, decorate with blanched, whole almonds. A more delicate version is to use only chicken breasts, boned and sliced, with the sauce and rice. An exotic salad is made of peeled persimmons, sliced, and watercress. Serve wine.

ARROZ con POLLO or RICE with CHICKEN DON CHÚ-CHÚ

2 chickens, 4 lbs. each
1 cup chopped onions
Whole green olives
Chopped parsley
1 cup olive oil
2 cloves garlic, minced
Salt, pepper, saffron
Paprika
Pimiento strips
2 cups raw white rice

Serves 8. Use necks, backs, gizzards for broth. Cut rest of chicken into serving pieces (or use thawed frozen chickens, cut for frying). Season and brown lightly in olive oil, adding onions and garlic. Transfer to iron kettle or earthenware cooking pot. Add 5 cups chicken broth (canned chicken broth may be used to augment amount). Cook slowly on top of stove, pot covered, until chicken is almost done. Add rice and 1 tsp. dissolved saffron. Continue to cook slowly, covered, until liquid is absorbed and rice dry and fluffy. Taste for seasoning without breaking rice. Add whole, unpitted green olives. Serve on hot platter, decorated with chopped parsley and pimiento strips.

Cut-up peeled bananas, fried in butter and combined with cooked frenched stringbeans (bright green), are a colorful tropical side dish. This is my favorite way to cook this classic Spanish dish. It was always cooked like this at our "Casa de Caoba" in Santo Domingo.

There are variations of this *sabroso* Latin favorite. In Cuba, the liquid used to cook the sautéed chicken and rice is beer, and the seasoning is "bijou," instead of saffron. In Puerto Rico, tomato paste, tomatoes, green peas, capers, orégano, and *achiote* (a locally grown red seed) are added to the chicken and rice. Ducks are often used instead of chicken (see Mexican section). The dish is then called

Arroz con Pato. In the Dominican Republic, the expression "patos de la Florida" refers to the American tourists who fly there, even as do the ducks from Florida to feed upon the rice fields on the island of Haiti.

PALOMAS SILVESTRES or WILD DOVES or SQUABS

6 wild doves or squabs
1/2 cup chopped onion
6 tbsps. butter
Paprika, salt, pepper
1/2 cup green pepper, seeded and shredded
2 cups cooked brown rice
1/2 cup stuffed olives
1 cup canned, or sautéed fresh mushrooms, sliced
2 cups dry red wine
Rosemary, sage
Minced parsley, chives
Light rum or brandy
Worcestershire sauce

Serves 6. Dress and clean doves or squabs, one to a person. Sauté onion and green pepper in half the butter. Add rice, olives, mushrooms, and seasoning. Stuff birds with this mixture, roast in uncovered pan. For the first 10 minutes, roast at 450°, then continue at 350° for 30 minutes more, basting with rest of butter added to 2 cups dry red wine. Length of time will depend on size of bird; it must be cooked through. This same dressing may be used to stuff wild ducks and guinea hens.

Brown birds quickly under broiler before serving. Make a sauce from drippings, adding crumbled rosemary, sage, parsley, and chives. Worcestershire sauce and a shot of rum or brandy lifts it to an epicurean dream come true. Heat sauce and pass separately. Extra cooked brown rice may also be served. Top off this fantasy with a tangerine ice and coconut macaroons.

TORTILLA de ARROZ or RICE OMELET

6 eggs, separated
Salt, pepper
Saffron, powdered
2 tbsps. butter
6 tbsps. milk
1 cup boiled rice

Serves 4-6. Add the milk and a good pinch of saffron to egg yolks, beat with salt and pepper. Add this mixture to rice, then fold in the stiffly beaten egg whites. Heat omelet skillet, add butter, let melt on sides and bottom. Pour in egg mixture and cook on top of stove until puffy. Put in moderate oven 325° and cook until top is nicely browned. Decorate with watercress and radish roses. With this, pass a sauce dish of creamed, sherried seafood to make a lovely luncheon dish.

HAITIAN HIGHLIGHTS

■■■A gourmet's haven is for the finding in unspoiled Haiti. The Haitian landscape of mountains, sea, and sky lends itself to exotic effects ... there nothing seems exaggerated. Champagne living on a limeade income are Haiti, Martinique, and Guadaloupe, that is, for the tourist! The two latter islands are still French-owned, but Haiti is an independent republic. How easy to slip from being an astute gourmet to a gloating gourmand on these French-Creole islands. But we relished every tempting mouthful and you will also. It is all irresistibly delicious, with an abundance of seafood, tropical fruits, and the best rice dishes ever to come out of a big *chodiè* (cauldron) over glowing *chabo* (charcoal).

RIZ à la CAMPAGNE or COUNTRY RICE

4 lbs. bacon, cubed
2 green peppers, chopped
Snipped parsley
10 onions, minced
8 cups canned tomatoes
Garlic salt, pepper, marjoram
2 cups sliced mushrooms
16 cups cooked white rice (4 lbs. raw rice)

Serves 30. Cut bacon into cubes. Cutting straight across a pound of sliced cold bacon (packaged, in U.S.) simplifies the task. Fry in huge skillet. When cooked, drain on brown paper. Brown onion and green peppers in some of the bacon fat. Add bacon, tomatoes, mushrooms, slightly undercooked rice, seasonings, and parsley. Stir with fork. Cover and steam until well heated.

As you can see, this amount will serve a big crowd. In Haiti, it is the *pièce de résistance* at the native *bamboches* (good-time gatherings) held outdoors. It is also an inexpensive addition to the buffet party. This is called *un diner debout* by the Haitian élite, who have adopted this *service modern,* bequeathed them by the American Marine Occupation, along with the cocktail party.

In Haiti the languages are French and a soft Creole, and both are represented in the excellent native cuisine—Frenchlike but mixed with a profusion of tropical produce.

You will love these still unspoiled islands which blend Creole with sophistication and mysticism. The haunting music, throbbing drums in the hills, and exciting outdoor *fêtes* are quite different in these French-African inspired isles. So why not hop a plane and visit these colorful Caribbean countries with their constant, cooling trade winds?

HAITIAN RICE and BEANS

1 lb. red or pinto beans
4 strips bacon
Thyme
Herb seasoning
Salt and pepper
Fresh lime juice
1 lb. white rice
2 minced cloves garlic
2 chopped onions
1 chopped sweet red pepper
2 cups cut-up ham

Serves 16. Do not pre-soak beans. The pinto bean comes nearest to the Haitian red bean, although the Congo bean is also close. Both the beans and the rice are packaged in 1-lb. sizes in he U.S. Fill a 4-qt. Dutch oven with 3 qts. salted water, bring to a boil, add washed beans, cut-up raw bacon or salt pork, minced garlic, chopped onions, and red pepper. If ham is raw, add now. Depending upon what the family can afford, any variety of meat may be added. Little sausages are favorites and are added during last part of cooking. Add 1 tsp. herb seasoning with ½ tsp. fresh or dried thyme in beginning. You may add more seasonings later on. Boil slowly, covered, until beans are almost soft. This takes about 3 hours of gentle simmering. Add 1 cup hot water each hour to keep liquid up to original water line. Stir with wooden spoon frequently from bottom. Slow charcoal heat is the best method. This is usually cooked outdoors under palm trees in a *chaudière* (iron cauldron) over live coals kept at an even temperature. The aroma is enticing indeed down there in Haiti.

When beans are almost tender, add the rice, making sure there is enough liquid (almost up to top of kettle). Simmer, covered, until rice is tender and liquid absorbed. Season with juice of fresh green lime to taste. **The amount** given in this recipe will vary according to appetites. If it is all there is on the menu, it is apt to be consumed very soon! When reheating, add water and more seasonings. Be careful not to scorch.

■

DI-RI et DJON-DJON or RICE and MUSHROOMS

Serves 8. This is the classic Haitian dish of Rice and Mushrooms. The measurements are 1 cup of sun-dried, black, native mushrooms, 2 cups white rice, and 4 cups water. Take half the water and let mushrooms come to a boil. Remove from stove, allow to steep, covered. Strain, saving the black water. Press the mushrooms with your fingers to extract all the choice *noir-noir* (black water), add this to the first cooking water. Add the chopped mushrooms (which resemble black tea when finely minced) to the **other** 2 cups of still "white" water with a spoon of bacon drippings, some chopped ham, and the usual nuance of crumbled wild thyme, salt, pepper, paprika, and majoram. Add black water, then the washed raw rice. Start off at high heat, reduce to simmer, and cook about 30 minutes, covered. A gourmet's dream is *accompli* at the first taste of this creole dish. Dried Chinese mushrooms may be used instead of the Haitian ones.

As a dessert for this tempting one-dish meal, try red bananas, roasted in their skins, peeled, then covered with a sauce made from chopped *marrons glacés* and rum. Light the sauce just at serving time. The combination brings forth exclamations of delight. Try this sauce on coconut ice cream!

RIZ à L'AVOCAT or RICE and AVOCADO

4 cups chicken broth
1 chopped onion
Marjoram
2 avocados
Chopped parsley
2 cups white rice
1 clove garlic
Salt to taste
Small cooked shrimp
Chopped pimiento
Fresh lime juice

Serve 6. Boil the chopped onion, garlic, and marjoram in chicken broth until onion and garlic are soft. There should be 4 cups broth in which to cook the rice. Add salt and chopped pimiento. Cook rice slowly, covered, until flaky. When ready to serve, heap in a mound on round platter. Decorate with cubed, peeled avocado, sprinkled with fresh lime juice and salt, and small, cooked pink shrimps. Sprinkle with parsley.

■

SHISH KEBAB and RICE, DRAMATIC

For a rather unusual dinner party, like the one we attended at the home of the French Chargé d'Affaires in Port-au-Prince, Haiti, prepare kebabs by cutting 1-inch squares from a leg of *cabrit* (young native goat) or a leg of lamb, uncooked. If preferred, the meat can be cooked first. Marinate in *orange sur* (which is the sour orange of Haiti) or substitute grapefruit juice, unsweetened. Add olive oil, chopped onion, garlic, chives, fresh mint, sage, brandy, and orégano in discreet amounts. Soak in this aromatic mixture overnight in refrigerator. Salt and pepper before putting on skewers to be broiled over a fire.

On the occasion which I am now recalling, a very dramatic effect was created by broiling the kebabs on oiled fencing foils, which our French host thought quite amusing. And it was. The squares of meat were put on the foils alternately with cubes of onions and egg plant. After the meat was broiled, it was brushed with warmed brandy, set afire, and served immediately.

There was a huge full moon over the swimming pool where we were being regaled. The kebabs were served hot on fluffy, dry rice, whose very blandness invited the exciting flavor contrast of the marinated meat. Champagne, native tom-toms throbbing in the perfumed night air—what a setting for dramatic menus!

■

RICE SALAD

Rice is served with much success as a salad in the French West Indies. The Haitians always cook their rice *bien grainnin*—each grain well detached one from the other, as they would say in their native patois. The local custom is to season cold boiled rice with vinegar, dry mustard, red pepper, and salt. Caper-dotted mayonnaise decorates the rice mound, with sliced green olives, fresh pineapple slices, quartered hard-cooked eggs, and tomato wedges to enhance the offering. A comprehensive rice dish is often created from the leftovers of a dinner party, and formed into *une salade terrifique* the next day. A bit risky to leave an uninhibited cook alone in the cuisine to concoct a Haitian *salade de riz!*

CASSEROLE MACÉDOINE

1 cup mushrooms
2 cups consommé
2 cups cooked rice
2 cups cooked ham
1/2 cup canned milk
Salt, nutmeg
3 tbsps. flour
3 tbsps. butter
1 cup canned petits pois (green peas)
2 tbsps. brown sugar
1/2 cup sherry
Cinnamon

Serves 8. Sauté canned, sliced mushrooms in butter. Remove mushrooms, add flour and consommé, and make a smooth sauce. Return mushrooms, add cut-up ham and the petits pois, drained. Put in buttered casserole; correct seasonings. Make a "crust" with the buttered, salted, cooked rice, mixed with milk, brown sugar, nutmeg, cinnamon, and sherry. Bake at 400° until light brown on top. Serve with fresh tropical fruit salad, such as pineapple, mangoes (or peaches), and bananas. Glasses of well-chilled *vin rosé* are in order. This light pink luncheon wine need not be an expensive imported brand here in the U.S., as California vineyards are now producing an excellent rosé wine at very modest cost. It adds a festive note to any occasion without impairing the budget. *Bon santé!*

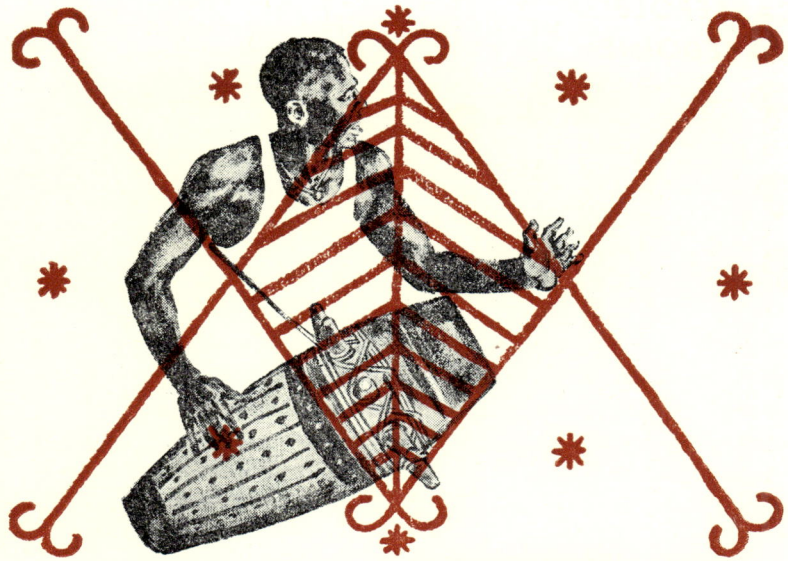

JAMAICAN SUCKLING PIG

■ ■ ■ Jamaica, that fabulous West Indian resort! Montego Bay is a continuous stretch of white coral beaches softly caressed by warm turquoise waters. When there is glamour and luxury, fine food usually follows.

Our idea of luxury, however, is not in hotels but on the far-flung wilderness of tropical beaches, lonely with a savage beauty. Huge combers break. Dashing into them is excitingly dangerous. Dripping and exhilarated, you approach a bronzed suckling pig which has turned on its bamboo spit for succulent hours! This is dining *au naturel*.

Unfortunately, most of us lead sheltered lives far away from coconut palm groves. Cooking is far easier done at home. It is impossible for most of us to dash off to a distant Caribbean island to prepare and roast a plump piglet under the stars. As a wonderful substitute, I will furnish you with this wholly excellent and realistic recipe, cleverly developed by the makers of Reynolds Wrap, who have given me permission to use it here. It is actually cooked and served this novel way at Shaw Park, a famous Jamaican resort. The foil method of roasting is exceedingly simple and most effective.

The perfume of little white trumpets, better known as stephanotis, jasmine, and tuberoses fill the night air in Jamaica. The fragrance of tropical blooms always seems sweeter after dark. Waves splash against the rocks in the distance, their misty spray dimly visible.

That's Jamaica! And now to the festive dish of this magic island.

■

JAMAICAN ROAST SUCKLING PIG with RICE STUFFING

8- to 12-lb. suckling pig
1¼ cups rice
1 pound fresh, delicately flavored sausage meat
Liver from the pig
1/4 pound butter
3 small onions, chopped
1 cup chopped celery
1 sweet red pepper, chopped
1/4 teaspoon thyme
1/4 teaspoon rosemary
2 teaspoons salt
3 small eggs, beaten

Serves 8–12. Roast Suckling Pig is a spectacular and delicious pièce de résistance for a buffet or party. It is easier to prepare than a turkey. The meat is almost fat free, very tender, and delicately flavored.

Order the piglet from the butcher several days ahead. It should not be larger than 12 pounds after dressing or it will be too large to get in the average home oven. Have the eyes, tongue, and feet removed at the market.

Singe to remove hair and scrape with a dull knife to remove bristles. Scrub the skin with a stiff brush and pat dry. Rinse the cavity, pat dry, and season with salt.

Cook rice. Sauté the sausage meat, breaking it apart, until a very light brown. Remove the meat and add the liver from the pig. Sauté until lightly cooked. Discard the sausage fat and add the butter to the pan. Add, one at a time, the onion, celery, and sweet pepper. Sauté until just tender, but not brown. Put the liver through the food chopper and add to rice. Add sautéed vegetables also and toss lightly with a fork. Add seasonings and taste. Since sausage contains a good amount of sage and other spices, only a limited amount of additional spices are necessary. Moisten with the beaten eggs until mixture clings together. Pack very lightly into piglet.

Close up the opening by sewing with a large needle and soft string.

Pull the front feet forward and tie together. Pull the hind feet backwards and tie together, if there is room in pan; otherwise pull forward. Crush foil to make a firm ball and place in mouth to keep it open. Cover the ears with small pieces of foil. Place the piglet on a large sheet of heavy duty aluminum foil. Rub skin with a cut lime and brush all over with melted butter. Season with salt and pepper. Bring the foil up over the back, overlapping it about 3 inches. Fold up the foil at head and feet ends.

Place the wrapped pig in a large, shallow pan and roast in a pre-heated hot oven (450°) allowing 2½ hours for an 8- to 10-pound pig and 3 hours for a 10- to 12-pound pig. At the end of this time, reduce heat to 375°, and open and turn back the aluminum foil. Baste with melted butter and continue roasting for 15 minutes or until skin is a beautiful golden brown.

Remove lacings and ties from piglet and transfer to a plank covered with foil. Remove foil ball from mouth and insert a lime or small mango. Use maraschino cherries for the eyes and decorate with parsley and fruit. In carving the piglet, start in center and cut right down through, serving complete slice to each person. If served as an hors d'oeuvre, slices can be cut in tidbit pieces on separate plate. Legs are removed and sliced. Ladle mango rum sauce over each serving.

Mango Rum Sauce

Lifting carefully, pour the juice remaining in the foil-wrap into a saucepan. Simmer and skim off fat. Add chicken broth to make 2 cups. In a separate pan place ¼ cup lime juice and 4 tablespoons granulated sugar. Cook together until a rich brown caramel is formed, then add to broth. Thicken just a little with cornstarch mixed with water. Add salt to taste.

When ready to serve, have mango cut in small slices or balls in a silver sauce-boat or other heat-proof server. Heat the rum in a small decorative saucepan. Pour hot sauce over mango and bring to the table with the rum. Pour a little of the rum in the sauce ladle and ignite with match and add to sauce. Add remaining rum, pouring it into ladle, then floating it on sauce. When rum has burned for a few minutes, ladle sauce over and over to blend delicious flavors. De luxe and delightful!

BARBADOS BOUNTY

■■■ In beautiful Barbados, luxurious beach houses, moonlight, and tropical fragrances blend into an assured retreat from the commonplace. We were enchanted by the best the Federated British West Indies had to offer in exciting party fare. On this island, everyone, including the British, prefers spiced dishes, but subtly and delicately keyed, not biting with chili as in Mexico. This addiction to spices and herbs turns their creole cuisine into a truly venturesome art, like adding a flash of unusual color to a dark costume ... or a spicy sauce to plain boiled rice!

Life is to the Barbadian native what it was to the dreamy Greek lotus eaters, and the flying fish has become as symbolic as the lotus. From this lovely island where we have spent so many happy vacations, I have saved these special "receipts" given me by British friends. Many of the early settlers in Charleston, S. C., came from Barbados, bringing their native dishes to our country.

In the Barbados, delicate, pearl-hued flying fish, exciting huge turtles, and native conch are the specialties of the island. These are hard to come by, so I have given the equally popular Finnan Haddie as a substitute. Rice needs no substitute and is eaten three times a day by the natives, and almost as often by the British colony.

RICE and TOMATO PIE

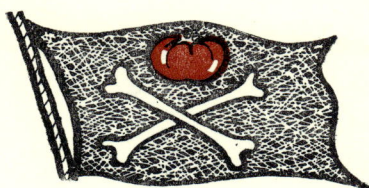

1 cup white rice
Lime juice
Butter; curry powder
Salt and pepper
1 small can tomatoes
Some chopped chives
Worcestershire sauce
Grated sharp cheese

Serves 6. Cook the rice in water with salt, lime juice, and butter to taste. Turn heat low, cover, and simmer until almost done. Drain, put in oven to dry out. Add a little curry powder, stir lightly with a fork. Arrange rice in a greased pie pan, making a hole in the center. Fill this with stewed tomatoes, drained and seasoned with chopped chives, Worcestershire sauce, salt, and pepper. Scatter grated cheese over top. Put under broiler to brown to a golden hue. This is very good with fish or seafood in any form. Broiled fish, with fresh lime juice and butter, is the most delicate of all. This is the way most *'badians* prefer their beloved flying fish.

CREOLE RICE

2 cups white rice
4 cups tomato or vegetable juice
1 green pepper, chopped
1 small onion, chopped
Boiled ham, cut up

Serves 6. Boil the rice in the tomato or vegetable juice. When cooked, add the other ingredients, all sautéed. Mix with a silver fork, put in buttered baking dish, dot with butter, and brown in oven. This is also known as "red rice." It is a fine partner for a fluffy mushroom, shrimp, or cheese omelet, served with marmalade made of limes and oranges.

CREAMED FINNAN HADDIE on RICE NESTS

2 lbs. finnan haddie fillets
1 grated onion
A shake of Tabasco sauce
Sherry
Butter
2 cups cream sauce
1 can sliced mushrooms
1 tsp. Worcestershire sauce
Salt, pepper, cayenne, dry mustard
2 cups cooked rice

Serves 6. Soak fillets several hours, drain, remove skins and bones. Break into medium pieces. Prepare a cream sauce (or use 1 can cream of mushroom soup, mixed with ½ can milk), add canned mushrooms and liquid, onion, and seasoning. Taste for salt. Add sherry last, according to amount desired. Place fish and sauce alternately in a buttered baking dish, resting in a pan of water. Bake 1 hour at 325°, then turn off heat. Keep covered in oven until serving time, as it must be very hot. It is served on nests of dry, white rice. This is fine for a Sunday breakfast or bruncheon, with papaya (or other melon), sprinkled with fresh lime juice, as the "eye opener."

■

BARBECUED PULLETS with RICE

Fat pullets
2 cups sautéed, chopped onions
2 tbsps. salt
1 tsp. each ground ginger and celery seed
1/2 tsp. cayenne pepper
2 tbsps. Worcestershire sauce
6 cloves garlic, minced
2 cups herb vinegar
1 tsp. each nutmeg and allspice
2 cups canned tomatoes
2 cans stale beer
Sugar to taste

Caramelize enough sugar to darken the stale beer. Add the mixture listed above, and bring to a boil. When it cools, add 1 tbsp. sugar or more, to taste. You can brew a lot of the sauce at one time, as it keeps well. Split in halves the plumpest young pullets you can acquire. Soak them in the barbecue sauce; broil over red coals, basting frequently; do not be afraid to scorch a little. Use a celery stalk for a barbecue brush. This piquant sauce is excellent on spareribs or suckling pig. Always serve slices on dry, cooked rice to absorb the rich juices.

SHRIMP and RICE PIE

Pie crust
3 hard-cooked eggs
Butter
Shrimp
Lime juice
Pepper, salt, cayenne
Rosemary, tarragon
Cooked white rice
Dry white wine

Serves 6. Line the sides of a Pyrex pie plate with pastry. Hard cook 3 eggs, rub the yolks to a smooth paste with 2 tbsps. butter, and chop the whites. Put a layer of cleaned, cooked shrimp in the dish, scatter some of the seasonings over them, and squeeze fresh lime juice over all. Put a layer of rice over the shrimp, dot with butter, some chopped egg whites, and some of the yolk-butter. Fill the dish in this way. Pour a little white wine over it when the dish is full. Cover with cross-bars of pastry. Bake in 325° oven until crust is light brown.

This is a famous "receipt" dated 1879.

THE GENERAL'S DOUBLE LAMB CHOPS

Brown on both sides as many perfect double lamb chops as needed in oiled skillet. Transfer to shallow baking pan. On each salted and peppered chop, put 1 tbsp. raw rice, cover with a thick slice of Bermuda onion, next a slice of green pepper, 2 anchovy fillets, and top with a large mushroom cap. Add tomato or vegetable juice to pan and steam for about 1½ hours, in 325° oven. Make a sauce from drippings, season, and pass separately with extra cooked rice.

JUGGED RICE

Serves 6. Chop watercress, green onion tops, and young spinach leaves (in Barbados they use eddo leaves) to make 1 cup "green seasoning." Cook 2 cups "tree pidgeon pease" (or split green peas), previously soaked, in salted water to cover. Add ½ lb. cut-up salt pork. When peas are soft, drain, add green seasoning, white pepper, and butter and mash to a purée. Mix with 1 cup cooked, dry, flaky white rice, buttered and hot. Stir lightly and heat over hot water. This is the 'badian version of the usual Caribbean "rice and beans." Serve with cold, sliced mutton and pickled mangoes or peaches for luncheon.

CRACKLING VEAL with RICE, PICNIC STYLE

Have your butcher roll and tie a rump of veal. Insert garlic cloves and crushed bay leaves into crevices. Rub a mixture of half olive oil, half bacon fat, over outside; sprinkle dry mustard, salt, cracked pepper, cayenne, fresh lime juice, A-1 sauce, and basil generously on meat. Dot with whole cloves. Turn slowly on revolving spit over glowing charcoal until well done. Serve crackling pieces of meat on hot, boiled white rice. Allow ½ lb. per person. Beef, pork, or mutton (lamb) may be used.

TRINIDAD'S MELTING POT

■ ■ ■ From restful Barbados, we came to spend carnival time in lively Trinidad. A group of Calypso singers put us into a merry-making mood right away. The rhythm of these spontaneously composed parodies is tantalizing. Their steelband music, with throbbing drums made of oil tanks and pail lids, their flashy costumes and wild dances, all added to a gay experience for us. The Calypsonians sing in a basic tempo which has in it African, Spanish, and French, interspersed with the broadest of English accents, jotted with American slang. This in itself shows how many peoples have influenced and formed Trinidad. The population includes Negroes, Chinese, Portuguese, Venezuelans, Syrians, Dutch, and East Indians. Trinidad, a British Crown Colony since 1797, is now the chosen capital of the Federated British West Indies.

To our amusement, we were entertained during dinner by parodies about us. The Calypsonian's readiness to sing for his supper ran something like this:

> Men and gals walking all aroun'
> Don't know where their next meal will be foun'
> Idling with a toothpick between their teeth
> Making people think they jes' done eat
> Many another time in days of need
> They will sacrifice a breadfruit for a great
>   big feed
> So take a mahn like me
> Singin' this song on an empty bellie.

Keeping envious eyes on our curried chicken, with mock pathos they sang huskily:

> Mongoose, he go to white mahn's kitchen
> Dere he pick out de fattest chicken
> Stuff it down his front vest pocket
> Old sly Mongoose!

The local servants never take food from the icebox and cook at the same time. Every well-staffed kitchen has an "ice-box maid," who hands food from the refrigerator to the cook. They insist they will "catch the fever" if they cook and "fetch food out." Yet the climate is delightful. The natives are always laughing and friendly. This light-hearted ditty is *so* pat that I can't resist quoting it:

> Rice is good and meat is nice
> But Trinidad rum is all sugar n' spice.

■

Little oysters growing on the trunks of mangrove trees, and on the ends of their branches, are a great specialty in

Trinidad. Sir Walter Raleigh, who first sailed into the waters surrounding Trinidad in 1595, made note of these "oisters." Creamed and baked with cooked rice in scallop shells, they are delicious. Tree oysters are tiny and have a wild tang.

■

"QUICK OYSTERS" and RICE

1 cup shucked oysters, smallest size
Nutmeg, salt, mace
1 cup cream sauce
4 tbsps. sherry
Melted butter

Serves 4. Make a cream sauce (condensed cream of celery or mushroom soup gives a modern, but speedy note); add drained oysters, quickly curled in butter. Season, add sherry, and serve on cooked white rice, colored with turmeric.

■

CHICKEN PÉLAU

1 large chicken, cut up
1 tsp. sugar
4 cups chicken broth (or more)
2 cups raw rice
1/2 cup olive oil
2 each onions and tomatoes
Chives and thyme, minced
Salt, pepper
Chopped onion tops
1/4 cup chopped almonds

Serves 6. Brown chicken in hot oil, add onions and tomatoes, cut up, and all the rest of the ingredients excepting almonds and rice. This should be done in a large iron skillet. Cover and cook gently for 45 minutes. Add rice, with saffron or turmeric if yellow rice is desired. Cover and cook slowly for about 20 minutes more. At serving time, sprinkle chopped, blanched almonds over top.

■

CALLALU GUMBO

1 bunch eddo leaves, or 1 lb. fresh raw spinach
1/2 lb. salt pork
6 cleaned raw crabs, claws left whole
1 qt. soup stock
3 tomatoes, cut up
1 onion, chopped
Shallots or chives
Sherry
Assorted seasonings
Cooked white rice

Serves 6. Chop the spinach in wooden bowl with tomatoes, onion, shallots or chives. The assorted seasonings include a pinch of mace, 2 bay leaves, and ½ green pepper, chopped. Put these with the quartered raw crabs and whole claws into a big iron cauldron, placed outdoors over glowing charcoal. Add 1 quart soup stock and season with cayenne, Tabasco, curry powder, allspice, and nutmeg. Salt to taste. Simmer until crabs are cooked. Remove them. Use a swizzle stick to bring up a foam. When callalu is a creamy texture, replace crabs. Add sherry. Using lump crab meat instead of raw crabs is my way of preventing gashes caused by crab shells. Add flaky, hot rice to each deep soup plate. This gives the real substance.

LOBSTER ANGOSTURA

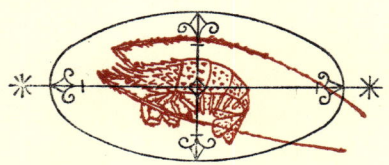

Lobsters
Butter
Angostura bitters
Salt, cayenne
Cooked rice
Canned milk
Sherry

Remove meat from the shells of as many cooked lobsters as you will require, cutting them in half. Melt sufficient butter, add lobster, cut in medium pieces. Cook a few minutes. Season with salt, cayenne, and bitters to taste. Combine the lobster with cooked rice. When heated through, add undiluted canned milk and sherry. Put the mixture back into the lobster shells, which have been cleaned. Broil until light brown. Garnish with lime wedges and preserved guava (or other fruit, such as watermelon), sliced and topped with cream cheese.

The Angostura Bitters Factory, which we visited outside the capital, Port-of-Spain, was founded in 1825. These bitters, whose formula is a secret of the inventor's family, were first used to prevent tropical fevers. Today, they spark up drinks, fruits, and gourmet cuisine.

■

CASSEROLE OF RICE

2 cups rice
1 tsp. saffron
1 tsp. salt
1/2 tsp. ginger
2 tbsps. butter
Grated cheese

Serves 6–8. Add the seasoning to a little more than 4 cups boiling water. Drop in raw rice slowly, reduce fire to a mere blue thread. Steam rice until it is almost done. Drain, put into a buttered casserole, sprinkle top with grated cheese, and bake until cheese is lightly browned.

1½ cups cooked rice
1 tbsp. butter
2 eggs
1 cup grated cheese
1/2 cup milk
Salt, pepper, paprika

RICE CHEESE IMPERIAL

Serves 6. Melt cheese and butter in casserole, add rice and lightly beaten egg yolks. Season, then add stiffly beaten egg whites last. Bake in a moderate oven about 30 minutes in a pan of warm water. Serve at once, as this is like a soufflé, and does not improve with waiting. But it is so delicate and delicious, it is well worth the trouble. Excellent as a luncheon dish by itself, or with the avocado halves filled with cold seafood, dressed with mayonnaise thinned with fresh lime juice and spiked with angostura bitters and curry powder. This is another version of the above-mentioned casserole of rice.

■

Onion
Garlic
Green pepper
Tomatoes
Salt, cayenne
Angostura bitters
Crayfish, prawn, or shrimp
Steamed rice

SHRIMP CREOLE CARIB

Make a creole sauce of the vegetables, seasoning to taste. Pour over cleaned, steamed crayfish, prawn, or shrimp. Steaming them in seaweed preserves their pristine, straight-from-the-sea flavor. Serve with steamed white rice. Strips of anchovy and pimiento, avocado slices, and fresh pineapple fingers, soaked in rum, top this tropical offering. In Trinidad, avocados are called zavocods.

HAM BANANA ROLLS

6 red bananas
1 tsp. mustard
2 tbsps. butter
6 slices boiled ham
1 tsp. horseradish
Parmesan cheese
Fried saffron rice
Rum

Serves 6. Peel the bananas, spread the ham slices with mustard and horseradish, and roll around bananas. Secure with toothpicks. Place in shallow baking dish, cover with melted butter and grated Parmesan cheese, and broil under broiler. Turn the rolls carefully once, so that they will brown on both sides. Have a platter of hot, crisply fried, saffron rice ready. On it place the rolls, pour rum over all. At table light the rum. Such a pretty sight!

CALYPSO CURRIED CHICKEN

2 frying chickens, cut up
2 cups chicken broth
1 piece ginger root
1 tbsp. lime juice
Vegetable oil
3 tbsps. curry powder
1 tbsp. cornstarch
2 cups coconut milk
One of each: chopped carrot, peeled apple, onion, garlic clove
Hot rice border

Serves 6. Sauté chicken in hot oil in heavy skillet. When golden, transfer to earthenware casserole. To remaining oil, add vegetables with curry powder and cornstarch. Stir over low heat. When thickened, strain and pour purée over seasoned chickens. Add ginger root, removing it before serving. There should be 2 cups chicken broth, which forms a sauce with the vegetable-curry purée. Cook slowly on top of stove until chickens are tender. Add coconut milk and taste to see if more curry powder, salt, and white pepper are needed. Continue simmering, adding fresh lime juice at the last. Serve curried chicken surrounded with a border of the white rice. Mango chutney is the only necessary "extra."

AVOCADO HALVES with CURRIED CRAB

Fill the halves of this tropical fruit with curried crab, lobster, shrimp, or chicken, using any of the recipes I have given. Add a few drops of angostura bitters to each serving. Place the unpeeled, filled halves in a baking dish in some water. Cover with a sheet of tinfoil. In Trinidad we used banana leaves. Bake at moderate temperature until curried mixture is heated through. Sprinkle inside and around edge of each avocado with fresh lime juice to prevent discoloration. Do not overcook. The bland flavor of the avocado is an excellent mediator for the sharp curry. Serve with Casserole of Rice (see recipe, page 176).

East Indians form one-third of the population of Trinidad, adding their Hindu costumes and love of curries to the West

Indian scene. While in Port-of-Spain, I talked with the English-speaking East Indians living there. Their cooking secrets added to those of the Trinidadians create a challenging cuisine. This is indeed where the East Indian meets the West Indian. Throughout, rice becames the common meeting ground, gastronomically speaking.

The British favor curried dishes in the West Indies as much as they once did in the East Indies.

"The condiments add variety, the curry adds spice, and the rice adds life!"

CURAÇAO'S CUISINE

■ ■ ■ We found excellent Dutch and Indonesian food served in seventeenth-century settings at several taverns in Curaçao. Willemstad, the capital, is more typically Dutch than any other city in the Netherlands West Indies. Everything is so clean, even the sea breeze smells scrubbed.

Many of the favorite dishes given in the Javanese chapter are duplicated in Curaçao, such as Nasi Goring (Fried Rice), curries, and satés (skewered meats). These Far Eastern favorites are served as often as the creole ones. All their islands, such as Aruba and Bonaire, and of course Curaçao, have a most friendly air. The cuisine is varied, since there is an Oriental as well as a European colony. You certainly get your money's worth in these Dutch Antilles in diverse ways. Tourists go for liquor and liqueurs. The locally made curaçao liqueur is internationally popular. Its special flavor is due to the addition of an extract from a small native orange. Holland gin and beer are much in demand but native rum still predominates.

STUFFED EDAM CHEESE

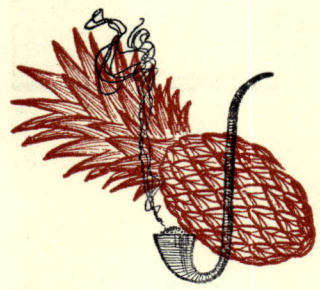

1 Edam cheese
1½ cups boiled, boned fish
1 onion, minced
2 ripe tomatoes, peeled and chopped
2 eggs
1½ cups cooked rice
1/4 cup raisins or currants
2 tbsps. sour pickles, chopped
10 stuffed olives, chopped
Salt, red pepper

Serves 8. Carefully cut top from a 3 lb. Edam cheese. Scoop out cheese, leaving about ½ inch shell. Soak in cold water to cover for 1 hour, then remove red rind by gently scraping with a small knife. Mix fish, onion, and tomatoes. Season to taste with salt and red pepper. Cook in melted butter until lightly browned. Beat eggs until foamy. Add rice; the scooped-out cheese, grated; the raisins or currants; pickles; and olives. Mix well. Combine the fish and rice mixtures. Press into hollowed cheese shell. Replace top. Place in a greased 2-qt. Pyrex baking dish, deep enough to hold the stuffed Edam cheese. Bake in a moderate oven, 350°, for about 1½ hours.

There is a little magic in this dish, according to my Dutch friend from Curaçao, and I find that he is right. Even though it is put into the oven whole, the outer shell melts and spreads to the sides of the baking dish. The result is a bubbly cheese rarebit. Serve on hot, dry white rice. It makes a fine breakfast dish with cold Amstel beer, fresh pineapple soaked in curaçao, and strong native coffee.

HAJACCAS or BANANA LEAVES STUFFED with CORNMEAL and MEATS

2 cups boned chicken, diced (may be canned)
2 cups cooked ham, diced
2 cups roast pork, cut finely
4 cups beef broth
2 cups raw rice
1 tsp. curry powder
1 cup chopped tomatoes
1 onion, minced
2 cloves garlic, minced
1 eggplant, peeled and diced
1/2 green pepper, chopped
1 small sweet red pepper, chopped
1 tbsp. butter

Serves 24. Mix the meats lightly and heat in the beef broth. Add the rest of the ingredients and simmer, covered, until rice is tender.

Now make a *mansa* (cornmeal paste) according to the following directions:

1½ cups cornmeal	Bouillon
1/2 lb. butter	Olives, chopped
2 tsps. salt	Capers
Shake of cayenne	Almonds
Pinch of thyme	Raisins
Milk	Prunes

Mix the first 7 ingredients above, using only enough milk and bouillon to make a good paste, not too soft.

Fold open the desired number of banana leaves (aluminum foil makes a fine substitute), wipe clean with a damp cloth, and put a spoonful of mansa on top of each leaf. Spread it out with a wet knife. Put some of the above-described rice mixture on top of the mansa on each leaf. Finish by placing a chopped olive, 2 capers, a sliced almond, a few raisins, and a cut-up prune on the rice mixture. Fold banana leaves like an envelope and tie closely with string. After preparing all the hajaccas in this way, put them in a large pan with boiling water. Steam for 2 hours.

These are similar to Puerto Rican *ayacas*. Each West Indian island calls the same specialty by a different name, although the same exotic abundance of fruits, fish, vegetables, and spices flourishes everywhere.

■

As one can readily see, creole cuisine is basically West Indian but it is interspersed with an East Indian influence in the British West Indies. This is because the British imported the East Indians to supplement labor on the vast sugar plantations.

During our delightful trip from the East to the West, have I proven that rice need never be dreary or monotonous? As rice is the staff of life to half the world, so is spice the magic touch we add to enliven our favorite food.

GLOSSARY OF SPICES

Name	Description	Uses
ALLSPICE (Pimento) **Spice**	Pea-sized fruit of a West Indian tree. Although a spice in its own right, flavor resembles a blend of cinnamon, nutmeg and cloves—hence its name.	*Whole*—pickling, meats, gravies, boiling fish. *Ground*—baking, puddings, relishes, some fruit preserves. *Try adding a dash to tomato sauce.*
ANISE **Seed**	Licorice-flavored fruit of a small plant grown in Spain, Syria, China, etc.	Good in cookies, candies, sweet pickles and as beverage flavoring. Sprinkle on coffee cakes, sweet rolls. *For anise cookies, just add 1/4 teaspoon ground anise to cookie batter.*
BASIL (Sweet Basil) **Herb**	Leaves and tender stems of an annual plant cultivated in western Europe.	An important seasoning in tomato paste and tomato dishes. Use in cooked peas, squash and string beans. Famed for use in turtle soup. *Sprinkle chopped basil leaves over lamb chops before cooking.*
BAY LEAVES (Laurel) **Herb**	Aromatic leaves of laurel tree from eastern Mediterranean countries. Used by ancient Greeks to crown heroes.	For pickling, stews, spice sauces and soups. Excellent for fish or chowder. Good with variety of meats, such as fricassee of kidney, heart or oxtail. *Add bay leaf, with whole peppercorns, to tomato sauce for boiled cod.*
BOUQUET GARNI (Herb Bouquet) **Blend**	Bunches of herbs and sometimes spices tied together or sewn in small cheesecloth sack and removed and discarded after cooking.	Usual combination consists of parsley, celery leaves, and onion and a sprig of thyme. Various combinations used for soups and stews. For example: *For lamb stew use parsley, thyme and clove.*

Name	Description	Use
CARAWAY Seed	Dried fruit of biennial plant grown in northern Europe, notably Holland. The important ingredient in the cordial, Kümmel.	Widely used in baking, especially rye bread. Good in sauerkraut, new cabbage, noodles and soft cheese spreads. Sprinkle over French-fried potatoes; on pork, liver, kidneys before cooking. *Sprinkle canned asparagus with caraway before heating.*
CARDAMOM Seed	Tiny brown seeds which grow enclosed in a small pod. Grown in India, Guatemala, Ceylon.	*Whole*—(in pod) used in Mixed Pickling Spice. *Seed*—(removed from pod) flavors demitasse. *Ground*—flavors Danish pastry, bun breads, coffee cakes. Improves flavor of grape jelly. *Sprinkle ground cardamom on iced melon for breakfast or dessert.*
CASSIA (Cinnamon) Spice	The bark of a tree grown in Indo-China, China, Indonesia. Cassia and cinnamon are botanically identical, although grown in different places. Cassia is used in this country as cinnamon because its flavor is stronger.	*Whole*—used in pickling, preserving, flavoring puddings, and stewed fruits. *Ground*—baked goods, mashed sweet potatoes, with sugar for cinnamon toast. *Use ground cinnamon in chocolate sauce for ice cream topping.*
CASSIA BUDS Spice	Dried unripe or ripe buds of tree from which cassia bark is obtained. Has rich flavor and high oil content.	*Used in pickling.*
CAYENNE (Red Pepper) Spice	Spicy small peppers. Most pungent of *capsicums*.	Meats, sauces, fish, egg dishes. The use of just the right amount of cayenne is the hallmark of the good chef. *Touch of cayenne plus 1/4 teaspoon paprika added to 2 or 3 tablespoons butter makes excellent sauce for vegetables.*

Name	Description	Use
CELERY SALT **Condiment**	Made by combining ground celery seed with salt.	Good with fish, boiled or fried eggs, potato, salad, salad dressings, tomato and kraut juices. bouillon. *Try celery salt as seasoning for any kind of croquette.*
CELERY SEED **Seed**	A minute seed-like fruit grown in many countries, especially France, India.	Excellent in pickling, salads, fish, salad dressings, and vegetables. *For a different flavor, add celery seed to braised lettuce (about 1/2 teaspoon to a head of lettuce).*
CHERVIL **Herb**	Leaf of herb that grows in many countries in the temperate zone.	Resembles mild parsley in flavor. Good in soups, salads, egg dishes, French dressing, fish, butter sauce for chicken. *Chop fine, then sprinkle over broiled fish before removing from broiler.*
CHILI POWDER **Blend**	Blend of phili ceppers and other spices.	Basic seasoning for Mexican cooking including chili con carne. Good in shellfish and oyster cocktail sauces, boiled and scrambled eggs, gravy and stew seasoning. *Good seasoning for ground meat or hamburgers.*
CINNAMON **Spice**	Aromatic bark of cinnamon tree, grown mostly in Ceylon.	See cassia.
CLOVES **Spice**	Nail-shaped bud of stately clove tree, grown in Indonesia, Madagascar, Zanzibar.	*Whole*—for pork and ham roasts, pickling of fruits, spiced sweet syrups. *Ground*—baked goods, chocolate puddings, stews, vegetables. *For a tastier meat stew add a small onion studded with 2 or 3 whole cloves.*

Name	Description	Use
CORIANDER Seed	Dried fruit of a small plant, resembling white peppercorn. Grown in Morocco, Argentina.	*Whole*—in mixed pickles, gingerbread batter, cookies, cakes, biscuits, poultry stuffings, mixed green salads. *Ground*—in sausage making, to flavor buns. *Rub ground coriander on fresh pork before roasting.*
CUMIN Seed	Small dried fruit resembling caraway in shape. Comes from Morocco, Cyprus, Syria, Iran. One of oldest known spices.	An ingredient in curry and chili powders. Available whole and ground. Good in soups, cheese, pies, stuffed eggs. *For canapés, mix chutney with snappy cheese and garnish with cumin seed.*
CURRY POWDER Blend	A blend of many spices. Basic to cookery of India.	Used in curry sauce, for currying eggs, vegetables, fish and meat. Try a dash in French dressing, scalloped tomatoes, clam and fish chowders. *Add 1 teaspoon to can of tomato soup.*
DILL Seed	Small dark seed of dill plant, imported from India.	Used for pickling, in cooking sauerkraut, salads, soups, fish and meat sauces, gravies, spiced vinegars, green apple pie. *Sprinkle dill seeds on potato salad, cooked macaroni or when cooking sauerkraut.*
FENNEL Seed	Small seed-like fruit with agreeable odor and aromatic sweet taste somewhat like anise. Grown in Europe, South America, Asia, Africa, Near East.	Popular in sweet pickles. Used in boiled fish, pastries, candies and liqueurs. *Add a dash to apple pie for an unusually good flavor.*
FINES HERBES (Fine Herbs) **Blend**	Fixed combinations of three or more herbs used to flavor certain dishes.	Herbs are mingled, finely chopped and placed in food just before serving. Used in many recipes. For example: *For pork dishes use about 1/2 teaspoon each of sage, basil and savory.*

Name	Description	Use
FENUGREEK Seed	Hard seed, strong and pleasant aroma. Member of pea family. The only leguminous herb. Native to Southern Europe, now grown also in Africa, India.	Used in some curry powder formulae, in mango pickle and green mango chutney recipes.
GARLIC SALT Condiment	Garlic powder with salt.	May be used in addition to or instead of plain salt in many dishes. Puts zest into tomato juice, any meat or vegetable dish, stews, French dressing or salads. *Season steaks with garlic salt before cooking.*
GINGER Spice	Root of a tuberous plant grown in Asia, Africa, West Indies.	*Cracked*—chutneys, conserves, pickling. Stew with dried fruits, apple sauce. *Ground*—gingerbread, cakes, pumpkin pie, Indian pudding, canned fruits, pot roasts and other meats. *Rub chicken inside and out with mixture of ginger and butter before roasting.*
MACE Spice	Fleshy growth between nutmeg shell and outer husk, orange-red in color. Flavor resembles nutmeg. Grown in Grenada, Indonesia, India.	*Whole* (called Blade)—excellent in fish sauces, pickling, preserving. Add a chopped blade to gingerbread batter. Good in stewed cherries. *Ground*—essential in fine pound cakes, contributes a golden tone and exotic flavor to all yellow cakes. Valuable in all chocolate dishes. *Use 1 teaspoon ground mace to 1 pint of whipped cream, cuts oiliness, increases delicacy.*
MARJORAM Herb	Herb of the mint family imported from France, Chile.	*Leaf*—delicious combined with other herbs in stews, soups, sausage, poultry seasonings, etc. Good in fish and sauce recipes. *Sprinkle over lamb while cooking for an excellent flavor touch.*

GLOSSARY

Name	Description	Use
MINT (DRIED) Herb	Strong, sweet flavor; grown in most of temperate zone. Only spearmint and peppermint used in spice trade.	Dried mint used for flavoring soups, stews, beverages, jellies, meat, fish, sauces etc.
MIXED PICKLING SPICE (Mixed Whole Spice) **Blend**	Assortment of a dozen or more whole spices.	Pickling and preserving of meats, vegetables, relishes, gravies, sauces. Also to perk up stews, drop bag of spices into stew and remove when properly flavored. *For a gourmet touch, add 1 tablespoon to boiling beets and cabbage.*
MUSTARD Seed	Small seed, widely cultivated. Domestic production supplies bulk of U.S. market, with additional imports from Europe and China.	*Whole*—used to garnish salads, pickled meats, fish and hamburgers. *Dry*—(also known as Mustard Flour)—meats, sauces, gravies. *Prepared*—(blended with other spices and vinegar, prepared mustard is the most popular U. S. condiment)—sandwiches, hot dogs, ham not the same without it. *Add 1/2 teaspoon dry mustard for each two cups of cheese sauce for macaroni.*
NUTMEG Spice	Kernel of the nutmeg fruit, grown in Grenada, India, Indonesia.	*Whole*—to be grated as needed. *Ground*—used in baked goods, sauces, puddings. Topping for eggnog, custards, whipped cream. Good on cauliflower, spinach. Sprinkle on fried bananas, on bananas and berries with cream. Best spice flavoring for doughnuts. *A pinch of nutmeg adds flavor to the crust for meat pie.*
ONION SALT Condiment	Mixture of ground dehydrated onions and salt.	Extremely handy for ever-ready use in place of fresh onions. Flavoring for meats, sauces, gravies—in any dish where onions are used. *Scalloped potatoes and hamburgers have a saucier flavor if seasoned with onion salt.*

GLOSSARY

Name	Description	Use
ORÉGANO **Herb**	An essential ingredient of chile con carne, orégano is grown mostly in Mexico and Italy. Increasing in popularity throughout U.S.	Good flavoring for pork dishes. Similar to marjoram in flavor but stronger. Fine seasoning for beef stews, meat sauces, gravies, omelet or boiled eggs. *Sprinkle into meat sauce for spaghetti.*
PAPRIKA **Spice**	A mild, heat-free member of the *capsicum* family.	Used as colorful red garnish for any pale foods. Important ingredient in Chicken Paprika and Hungarian Goulash. Used on fish, shellfish, salad dressings, vegetables, meats, gravies, canapés. *For an excellent canapé mix paprika with cream cheese and celery seed and serve on crackers.*
PARSLEY (DRIED) **Herb**	Widely cultivated, including U.S.A.	Often is packed as "Parsley Flakes." Used as seasoning and garnish. Flavors soups, salads, meat, fish, sauces and vegetable dishes. *For Spiced Potato Cakes made from leftover mashed potatoes, or to reheated mashed potatoes, try adding some parsley flakes, onion salt and paprika.*
PEPPER **Spice**	Small dried berry of vine. Whole pepper is known as peppercorn. Pepper is the world's most popular spice. White pepper is black peppercorn with outer pulp fibre material removed. Use fresh pepper; buy small quantities and replace often!	Adds a spicy tang to almost all foods. An absolute "must" in the kitchen and on the table. *Whole*—(Black and white) used in pickling, soups and meats. *Ground*—(Black and white) meats, sauces, gravies, many vegetables, soups, salads, eggs, etc. For curing Virginia-style hams. *Dash fresh black pepper in tossed green salad.*
POPPY **Seed**	Tiny seeds of poppy plant; about 900,000 to the pound. Best is blue-colored seed from Holland. Has a crunchy nutlike flavor.	Excellent as topping for breads, rolls, cookies. Also delicious in salads and noodles. Filling for pastries. *Add poppy seeds to buttered noodles and mix thoroughly.*

GLOSSARY **191**

Name	Description	Use
POULTRY SEASONING Blend	A mixture of herbs and spices.	For poultry, veal, pork and fish stuffings. Good with paprika for meat loaf. *For a delightful combination, add to biscuit batter to serve with poultry.*
PUMPKIN SPICE Blend	A ready-mixed blend of spices.	Provides just the right flavor note for pumpkin pie, for spiced cookies, gingerbread, breakfast buns. *French fry slices of raw pumpkin and dust lightly with pumpkin pie spice for a delicious "something new."*
ROSEMARY Herb	A sweet and fresh-tasting herb which looks like a curved pine needle. Grown in France, Spain and Portugal.	Use in lamb dishes, in soups and stews. Sprinkle on beef before roasting. Flavors fish and meat stocks. *Add a sprig of rosemary to boiled potatoes in the early stages of cooking.*
SAGE Herb	America's most popular herb. The best grows wild in Yugoslavia.	Particularly good with pork and pork products. Used in sausages, meat stuffings, baked fish and poultry. Excellent in salad greens. *Season Manhattan Clam Chowder with sage.*
SAFFRON Spice	The world's most expensive spice, yet a little goes a long way. Takes 225,000 stigma of a crocus-like flower to make a pound. Grown in Mediterranean area.	In baked goods. Most highly esteemed in "Arroz con Pollo," the rice-chicken dish of Spain. *To add golden color and delicious flavor to rice, boil pinch of saffron in water for a moment before adding rice.*
SAUSAGE SEASONING Blend	Blend of herbs and spices including white pepper, coriander and nutmeg.	Excellent ready-mixed seasoning for the home sausage maker. Used also in meat loaf, veal birds, etc. *Mix with batter to make an herb bun to serve with fresh ham and other roasted pork.*

Name	Description	Use
SAVORY Herb	Herb of the mint family, grown in many climates. Imported from France and Spain.	Combined with other herbs, makes an excellent flavoring for meats, meat dressings, chicken, fish sauces. *A pinch of savory gives a lift to scrambled eggs.*
SESAME Seed	Small, honey-colored seed imported from Asia, Near East, Central America.	A rich toasted-nut flavor when baked on rolls, breads and buns. Principal ingredient in Oriental candy, halvah. *Add to lightly cooked cold spinach which has been blended with soy sauce. Turn out of custard cup and top with grated raw beets or carrots.*
TARRAGON Herb	Anise-flavored leaf of perennial.	Used in sauces, salads, chicken, meats, egg and tomato dishes. The important flavoring of tarragon vinegar. *Just before taking broiled chicken out of oven, season and sprinkle with finely minced tarragon and serve with pan gravy.*
THYME Herb	Leaves and tender stems of garden herbs. Many varieties. Imported mostly from France and Spain. Has a strong, distinctive flavor.	Used in stews, soups and poultry stuffings. Excellent in clam and fish chowders, in meat and fish sauces, croquettes, chipped beef, fricassees. *Thyme and fresh tomatoes go together like hand and glove. Sprinkle thyme over sliced tomatoes in bed of lettuce, use vinegar and olive oil dressing, with salt and pepper.*
TURMERIC Spice	Root of the ginger family, orange-yellow in color. Important ingredient of curry powder, imported from India, Haiti, Jamaica.	Used as flavoring in prepared mustard, and is used in combination with mustard as flavoring for meats, dressings and salads. Used in pickling, Chow Chow and other relishes. *Try a little turmeric in creamed eggs, fish, seafood.*

Name	Description	Use
VANILLA Spice	Vanilla beans are dried, cured fruit of an orchid, native of Central America. Comes also from Africa and Far East.	Used mostly in pure extract form, for baking and desserts, candy, syrups.

INDEX

Admiral's Pacific Pork Chops, 65
Ajam Beseng, 32
Ajis Dulces Rellenos con Arroz, 145
Albondigas con Arroz, 130
Arroz Amarillo, 147
Arroz con Frijoles, 140
Arroz con Pato, 135
Arroz con Pescado, 146
Arroz con Pollo, 151
Arroz con Sardinas a la Carmen, 68
Arroz con Señoritas, 134
Arroz Verde, 144
Avocado Halves with Curried Crab, 179

Baked Fish with Almond Sauce, 130
Baked Wild Rice with Oysters and Shrimp, 120
Banana Leaves Stuffed with Cornmeal and Meats, 183
Barbecue
  Barbecued Pullets, 169
  Korean Chicken, 45
  Peri-peri Chicken, 112
  Sasaties, 113
  Saté or Skewered Meat with Rice, 32
  Shish Kebab, 158
Barbecued Pullets with Rice, 169
Batters and Breads
  Indian Fry Bread, 124
  Rice Griddle Cakes, 91
  Special Batter Bread, 93
  Tempura, 49
Beef
  Carne con Berenjenas y Arroz or Meat Loaf with Eggplant and Rice, 141
  Concha's Stew or Steamboat Hash, 83
  Kentucky Burgoo, 89
  Rice Ring Rio Grande, 82
  Sherried Beef Muffins con Arroz, 76

Beef (*continued*)
  Stroganov with Rice, 106
  Sukiyaki, 50
  Thursday Night Beef Stew, 70
Beef Stroganoff with Rice, 106
Bengal Curry of Mutton or Veal, 19
Breads. See Batters and Breads
Brown Rice with Spanish Sausages, 142
Browned rice, 133
Brunswick Stew, 110

California Pot Roast of Chicken with Burgundy and Rice, 63
Callalu Gumbo, 175
Calypso Curried Chicken, 178
Camarones Picantes con Arroz, 144
Caneton Montmorency, 110
Carne con Berenjenas y Arroz, 141
Casserole Macédoine, 160
Casserole of Hoppin' John, 92
Casserole of Rice, 176
Ceylonese Curry, 23
Cheese
  Rice, Imperial, 177
  Stuffed Edam, 182
Chicken. See also Fowl
Chicken and Rice, Valenciana, 37
Chicken with Vegetables, 42
Chicken Curry, Calcutta, 16
Chicken Curry California with Rice, 64
Chicken from Castile, 150
Chicken Curry with Rice, 32
Chicken Legs *Teriyaki* on Rice, 47
Chicken Pelau, 174
Chicken Pilaff, 104
Chicken Pilau, 95
Chick Peas and Rice, 149
Chili
  con Carne, 131
  Country Captain, 78
  Simple, and Rice, 80
  Sopa Seca, 131

Chinese Almond Chicken with Rice, 39
Chinese Chopped Shrimp and Vegetables with Rice, 40
Chorizos con Arroz, 142
Chutney
  Lord Napier's, 18
  Mimi's, 108
  Uncooked, 108
citrus salad, Carmel style, 61
coconut milk, 60
Concha's Stew, 83
Condiments
  Lord Napier's Chutney, 18
  Mimi's Chutney, 108
  Sambals, 17
  with California touch, 64
  with Hawaiian touch, 59
  Uncooked Chutney, 108
Country Captain, 78
Country Rice, 155
Coolie Tiffin, 41
Crab Meat and Rice *au Gratin*, 66
Crab Meat in Rice Patties, 62
Crackling Veal with Rice, Picnic Style, 171
Creamed Finnan Haddie on Rice Nests, 168
Creamed Rice and Mussels, 73
Creamed Rice Soup, 142
Creole Rice, 168
Cuban Picadillo and Fluffy White Rice, 101
Curried Casserole, Waikiki, 57
Curried Meat with Rice, 31
Curried Scallops, 112
Curry
  Ajam Beseng, 32
  Avocado Halves with Curried Crab, 179
  Bengal Mutton or Veal, 19
  Calypso Curried Chicken, 178
  Ceylonese, 23
  Chicken, and Rice, Calcutta, 16
  Chicken Curried California, 64
  Curried Casserole, Waikiki, 57
  Curried Scallops, 112
  East Indian Curried Shrimp, 20
  Gil Allen's Lamb, and Rice, 107
  Honolulu Lobster, 59
  in a Coconut, 56
  in a Hurry, 58
  Jachtschotel or Curried Meat with Rice, 31
  Malay Chicken, 27

Curry (*continued*)
  Sajoer, 29
Curry in a Coconut, 56
"Curry in a Hurry," 58

Del Monte Chicken with Rice, 74
Desserts
  Island Fruit Compote, 56
  Kuller-Pfirsich, 115
  Pineapple Ambrosia, 113
  red bananas with *marrons glacés* and rum, 157
Di-ri et Djon-djon, 157

East Indian Curried Shrimp, 20
Eggs
  and Rice before Reveille, 134
  Fried Rice with, 136
  Tortilla de Arroz or Rice Omelet, 153
Eggs and Rice before Reveille, 134
Escalloped Rice and Ham, 87
Estofado con Tomate y Arroz, 133

Feathered Rice, 80
"Fetteh and Rice," 98
Filetes de Pescado con Arroz, 143
Fish. *See also* Seafood
Fish and Rice Kedgeree, 24
Fish with Seasoned Rice, 146
Fish with Rice, 136
Fluffy White Rice, Cuban Style, 102
Fowl
  Arroz con Pato or Rice with Duck, 135
  Arroz con Pollo or Rice with Chicken *Don Chú-chú*, 151
  Avocado Halves with Curried Crab (or chicken), 179
  Barbecued Pullets with Rice, 169
  California Pot Roast of, 63
  Calypso Curried Chicken, 178
  Caneton Montmorency, 110
  Chinese Almond Chicken, 39
  Chicken and Rice, Valenciana, 37
  Chicken with Vegetables, 42
  Chicken Curry, Calcutta, 16
  Chicken Curry California with Rice, 64
  Chicken Legs *Teriyaki* on Rice, 47
  Chicken Pelau, 174
  Chicken Pilaff, 104
  Chicken Pilau, 95

Country Captain, 78
"Curry in a Hurry," 58
Fowl (*continued*)
   Brunswick Stew, 110
   Del Monte Chicken and Rice, 74
   Estofado con Tomate y Arroz or Stewed Chicken with Tomatoes and Rice, 133
   Hajaccas or Banana Leaves Stuffed with Cornmeal and Meats, 183
   Imaginative Chicken, 71
   Kentucky Burgoo, 89
   Korean Chicken, 45
   Malay Chicken, 27
   Paella with Rice, 148
   Palomas Silvestres or Wild Doves or Squabs, 152
   Peri-peri Chicken, 112
   Pollo Castellano or Chicken from Castile, 150
   Royal Casserole, 36
   Sajoer Curry, 29
   Syrian Chicken and Rice, 104
Fried Peanuts, 30
Fried Rice, 33, 41
Fried Rice with Eggs, 136
Fried Wild Rice with Almonds, 120

Garbanzos y Arroz, 149
General's Double Lamb Chops, 170
Gil Allen's Lamb Curry and Rice, 107
Golden Rice, 27
Grecian Dolmas, 109
Green Casserole with Wild Rice, 123
Green Rice, 144
Green-rice Stuffed Peppers, 145
Gumbo Soup, 96

Haitian Rice and Beans, 156
Hajaccas, 183
Ham Banana Rolls, 178
Hearts-of-artichoke salad, 63
Herbed Wild Rice, 122
Honolulu Lobster Curry, 59
Huachinango Veracruzano, 128

Imaginative Chicken and Rice, 71
Indian Fry Bread, 124
Island Fruit Compote, 56
Italian Rice, Monterey, 72

Jachtschotel, 31

Jamaica Roast Suckling Pig with Rice Stuffing, 162
Jambalay aux Écrivisses à la Louisiane, 85
Jambalaya Lafitte, 86
Jellied Borscht, 105
Jugged Rice, 171

Keem, 44
Kentucky Burgoo with Rice, 89
Korean Chicken, 45
Kuller-Pfirsich, 115

Lamb
   General's Double, Chops, 170
   Gil Allen's Curry and Rice, 107
   Grecian Dolmas, 109
   Shish Kebab and Rice, 158
Langostinas y Arroz en Conchas, 146
Lightning Rice Dish, 72
Lobster Angostura, 176
Lord Napier's Chutney, 18

Malay Chicken Curry with Rice, 27
Mango Rum Sauce, 164
Meat. *See also* Beef, Lamb, Pork, Veal
   Cuban Picadillo, 101
   Jachtschotel or Curried Meat with Rice, 31
   Meat and Rice Casserole, Carmel, 69
   Meat Balls with Rice, 130
   Near Eastern Meat Balls, 103
   Rice Pie, 95
   Rice Ring Rio Grande, 82
   Sasaties, 113
   School Boat Stew, 116
   Skewered Meat with Rice, 32
Meat and Rice Casserole, Carmel, 69
Meat Balls with Rice, 130
Meat Loaf with Eggplant and Rice, 141
Mexican-Rice Stuffing, 129
Minced Indian-corn Balls, 31
Minced Shrimp Balls, 30
Mimi's Chutney, 108
Mushroom sauce, 76

Nasi Goring, 33
Near Eastern Meat Balls and Rice, 103

Okra Pilau, 95
Paella with Rice, 148
Pah Jook, 45
Palmito, 37
Palomas Silvestres, 152
Pescado con Arroz, 136
Peri-peri Chicken, 112
Pie
  Rice, 95
  Rice and Tomato, 167
  Shrimp and Eggplant, 96
  Shrimp and Rice, 170
Pilau of Seafood, 94
Poached Fish Fillets with Rice, 143
Pollo Castellano, 150
Pork
  Admiral's Pacific, Chops, 65
  Adobo, 35
  Casserole Macédoine, 160
  Escalloped Rice and Ham, 87
  Hajaccas or Banana Leaves Stuffed with Cornmeal and Meats, 183
  Ham Banana Rolls, 178
  Jamaica Roast Suckling Pig, 162
  Jambalaya Lafitte, 86
  Rice Topped with Spicy Cabbage, 67
  Vegetables with Ham, 42
Pork Adobo, 35
Prawn and Rice in Scallop Shells, 146

"Quick Oysters" and Rice, 174

"Red lettuce," 61
Red Rice, 91
Red Snapper, Veracruz, 128
Rempejeh, 30
Rice
  and Little Scallops, 134
  and Raisin Pudding, 66
  and Tomato Pie, 167
  Arabic, 99
  Arroz Amarillo or Yellow Rice, 147
  Arroz con Frijoles or Rice and Beans, 140
  Arroz con Sardinas a la Carmen or Rice with Sardines, 68
  Arroz Verde or Green Rice, 144
  Border, 35
  browned, 133
  Casserole of Hoppin' John, 92
  Casserole of, 176
Rice (*continued*)
  Chorizos con Arroz or Brown Rice with Spanish Sausages, 142
  Cheese Imperial, 177
  Creole, 168
  Cuban style, 102
  Di-ri et Djon-djon or Rice and Mushrooms, 157
  Escalloped, and Ham, 87
  Feathered, 80
  Fish and, Kedgeree, 24
  Fried, 33, 41
  Garbanzos y Arroz or Chick Peas and Rice, 149
  Golden, 27
  Griddle Cakes, 91
  Haitian, and Beans, 156
  in a Pineapple Shell, 56
  Jugged, 171
  Lightning, Dish, 72
  Mexican, Stuffing, 129
  Nasi Goring or Fried Rice, 33
  Pah Jook or Rice and Beans, 45
  Pie, 95
  Red, 91
  Ring, 21
  Riz à l'avocat or Rice and Avocado, 158
  Riz à la Campagne or Country Rice, 155
  Salad, 159
  Simple Chili and, 80
  Sopa Seca, 131
  Spanish, 70
  -stuffed Squash, 68
  stuffing, 163
  Surprise, 87
  Texas-style Mexican, 81
  Topped with Spicy Cabbage, 67
  Tortilla de Arroz or Rice Omelet, 153
  White, East Indian Style, 16
Rice and Beans, 45, 140
Rice and Little Scallops, 134
Rice and Avocado, 158
Rice and Mushrooms, 157
Rice and Raisin Pudding for Children, 66
Rice and Tomato Pie, 167
Rice Border, 35
Rice Cheese Imperial, 177
Rice, Cuban Style, 102
Rice Griddle Cakes, 91
Rice in a Pineapple Shell, 56

Rice Omelet, 153
Rice Pie, 95
Rice Ring, 21
Rice Ring Rio Grande, 82
Rice Salad, 159
Rice-stuffed Squash, 68
Rice stuffing, 163
Rice Topped with Spicy Cabbage, 67
Rice with Duck, 135
Rice with Chicken *Don Chú-chú,* 151
Rice with Sardines, 68
Rijsttafel, 29
Riñones en Jerez con Arroz, 145
Riz a la Campagne, 155
Riz à l'avocat, 158
Royal Casserole, 36

Sajoer Curry, 29
Salad
  citrus, Carmel style, 61
  hearts-of-artichoke, 63
  Palmito, 37
  Rice, 159
  "salata," 109
  Spanish slaw, 135
  Texas Onions de Luxe, 79
"Salata," 109
Salsa Ramón, 100
Sambal Goreng Oedang, 30
Sambals, 17
Sancocho, 139
Sasaties, 113
Saté with Rice, 32
Sauces
  Mango Rum, 164
  Montmorency, 111
  mushroom, 76
  Ramón, 100
  Sukiyaki, 52
  Tempura, 49
Sauce Montmorency, 111
School Boat Stew, 116
Seafood
  Arroz con Pescado or Fish with Seasoned Rice, 146
  Arroz con Sardinas a la Carmen or Rice with Sardines, 68
  Arroz con Señoritas or Rice with Little Scallops, 134
  Avocado Halves with Curried Crab, 179
  Baked Fish with Almond Sauce, 130

Seafood (*continued*)
  Baked Wild Rice with Oysters and Shrimp, 120
  Callalu Gumbo, 175
  Camarones Picantes con Arroz or Spicy Shrimp with Rice, 144
  Ceylonese Curry, 23
  Chinese Chopped Shrimp and Vegetables, 40
  Crab Meat and Rice *au Gratin*, 66
  Crab Meat in Rice Patties, 62
  Creamed Finnan Haddie on Rice Nests, 168
  Creamed Rice and Mussels, 73
  Curried Scallops, 112
  East Indian Curried Shrimp, 20
  Filetes de Pescado con Arroz or Poached Fish Fillets with Rice, 143
  Fish and Rice Kedgeree, 24
  Honolulu Lobster Curry, 59
  Huachinago Veracruzano or Red Snapper, Veracruz, 128
  Italian Rice, Monterey, 72
  Jambalaya aux Ecrivisses à la Louisiane, 85
  Jambalaya Lafitte, 86
  Langostinas y Arroz en Conchas or Prawn and Rice in Scallop Shells, 146
  Lobster Angostura, 176
  Minced Shrimp Balls, 30
  Nasi Goreng or Fried Rice, 33
  Paella with Rice, 148
  Pescado con Arroz or Fish with Rice, 136
  Pilau of, 94
  "Quick Oysters", 174
  Sambal Goreng Oedang, 30
  Seafood Deepfreeze, 114
  Shrimp and Eggplant Pie, 96
  Shrimp and Rice Pie, 170
  Shrimp Creole Carib, 177
  Stuffed Edam Cheese, 182
  Tokyo *Tempura* Shrimp, 48
  Wild Rice with Crab Meat, 119
Seafood Deepfreeze with Special Rice, 114
Sherried Beef Muffins *con Arroz*, 76
Sherried Kidneys with Rice, 145
Shish Kebab and Rice, Dramatic, 158
Shrimp and Eggplant Pie, 96
Shrimp and Rice Pie, 170
Shrimp Creole Carib, 177

Side Dishes. *See* Condiments
Simple Chili and Rice, 80
Skewered Meat with Rice, 32
Sopa de Arroz con Crema, 142
Sopa Seca, 131
Sopa Seca de Arroz con Huevos, 136
Soups
    Callalu Gumbo, 175
    Gumbo, 96
    Jellied Borscht, 105
    Sopa de Arroz con Crema or Creamed Rice Soup, 142
Spanish Rice, 70
Spanish slaw, 135
Special Batter Bread, 93
Special rice, 114
Spicy Shrimp with Rice, 144
Steamboat Hash, 83
Stewed Chicken with **Tomatoes** and Rice, 133
Stuffed Edam Cheese, 182
Sukiyaki and Rice, 50
Sukiyaki Sauce, 52
Surprise Rice, 87
Syrian Chicken and Rice, 104

Tempura Batter, 49
Tempura Sauce, 49
Texas Onions de Luxe, 79
Texas-style Mexican Rice, 81
Thursday Night Beef Stew with Rice, 70
Tokyo *Tempura* Shrimp with Rice, 48
Tomato Pilau, 95
Tortilla de Arroz, 153

Uncooked Chutney, 108

Veal
    Bengal Curry of, 19
    Crackling Veal with Rice, 171
    Riñones en Jerez con Arroz or Sherried Kidneys with Rice, 145
    Veal with Rice Ring, 75
    Wild Rice and Sweetbreads, 122

Vegetables
    Ajis Dulces Rellenos con Arroz or Green-rice Stuffed Peppers, 145
with Ham, 42
Arroz con Frijoles or Rice and Beans, 140
Chicken with, 42
Chinese Chopped Shrimp and, 40
Di-ri et Djon-djon or Rice and Mushrooms, 157
Garbanzos y Arroz or Chick Peas and Rice, 149
Green Casserole with Wild Rice, 123
Haitian Rice and Beans, 156
Jugged Rice, 171
Minced Indian-corn Balls, 31
Okra Pilau, 95
Pah Jook or Rice and Beans, 45
Shrimp and Eggplant Pie, 96
Texas Onions de Luxe, 79
Tomato Pilau, 95
Rempejeh or Fried Peanuts, 30
Rice-stuffed Squash, 68
Rice Topped with Spicy Cabbage, 67
Wild Rice and Mushroom Ring, 121
Vegetables with Ham, 42

White Rice, East Indian Style, 16
Wild Doves or Squabs, 152
Wild Rice
    and chicken livers, 122
    and Mushroom Ring, 121
    and Sweetbreads, 122
    Baked with Oysters and Shrimp, 120
    Fried with Almonds, 120
    Green Casserole with, 123
    Herbed, 122
    with Crab Meat, 119
Wild Rice and chicken livers, 122
Wild Rice and Mushroom Ring, 121
Wild Rice and Sweetbreads, 122
Wild Rice with Crab Meat, 119

Yellow Rice, 147